A FRAMEWORK FOR EXCELLENCE:

A RESOURCE MANUAL FOR NLP

CHARLOTTE BRETTO MILLINER

Preface by Dr. John T. Grinder

Grinder & Associates

Published by
Grinder & Associates
P.O. Box 67295
Scotts Valley, CA 95067

Master Distributor:
Metamorphous Advanced Product Services
A Division of Metamorphous Press, Inc.
P.O. Box 10616
Portland, OR 97296-0616

Editorial and Art Direction by Lori Vannorsdel
Printed in the United States of America

Library of Congress Cataloging-in-Publication Data

Milliner, Charlotte Bretto, 1953-
    A framework for excellence : a resource manual for NLP / Charlotte Bretto
Milliner ; preface by John T. Grinder.
       p.   cm.
    Includes bibliographical references and index.
    ISBN 0-929514-03-3 : $29.95
    1. Neurolinguistic programming.   I. Title.
BF637.N46M55   1997
158' .9--dc21   .   96-52560
                                                    CIP

DEDICATION

TO ALL OF US WHO ARE STUDENTS OF NLP

UPDATE REQUEST

I am interested in receiving information regarding updates to this resource manual and resource material on the new code.

(Please Print)   Name: ─────────────────────

                Address: ─────────────────────

                              ─────────────────────

Business Phone: ─────────────────────

    Home Phone: ─────────────────────

Mail to:

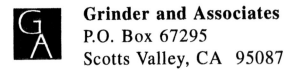 **Grinder and Associates**
P.O. Box 67295
Scotts Valley, CA 95087

CONTENTS

PREFACE
FOREWORD

PREFACE

Neuro Linguistic Programming (NLP) is an exploratory activity - a pursuit of patterns of excellence - this manual is a source of verbal description which when <u>acted upon by the reader</u> will materially assist the reader in developing the circuitry which will support their own exploration.

NLP, as I practice it, is a training ground for explorers not tourists. It is fundamentally an enterprise of the spirit. And as such, can never be captured by technique and never between the covers of a book. As Isadora Duncan said: "If I could say it, I wouldn't have to dance it." Bretto is attempting to point at something important in this Manual. Please look at what she is pointing to, not at her finger.

It is with a decidedly peculiar sensation that I write the preface to Charlotte Bretto's Reference Manual. There is no doubt in my mind that she has chosen well the set of exercises and supporting material which form the bulk of the Manual. The question implicit in the strange sensation I feel is quite simple: Will this work, the Resource Manual, promote orthodoxy? For example, looking at the section on Representational Systems, even though cleanly written, people have classified individuals as either visual, auditory or kinesthetic. Representational System preference changes based on context and some can last for as long as seven seconds. Take note as a practitioner what presuppositions, what perceptual filters, you chose and the effect they have on your behavior. Such shorthand promotes a certain kind of reification which tramples on the edge of orthodoxy - the single most persistent ghost pursuing my work.

Eric Hansen, in an amazing account of a personal quest involving crossing the jungles of Borneo (entitled <u>Stranger in the Forest</u>), discovers an astonishingly deep presupposition in his own thinking in contrast to the inhabitants of Borneo:

It used to frustrate me when they couldn't tell me how long it would take to arrive at a particular place that they knew well. The confusion arose from the fact that I was thinking in terms of miles and hours and they were thinking in terms of hunting. If there was a lot of game, a short distance could take a long time to cover because they would hunt. Equally, we could travel long distances quickly if there were no animals about or if they wanted to reach a place where they felt the hunting would be better. Their concept of distance was also dependent on mood or need. A destination "not too far away" could mean a five-day walk through difficult terrain to a friendly village where they could buy tobacco. A "long journey" might turn out to be a four-hour walk in the hated sunlight through flat farmland.

It was equally as difficult for them to understand my idea of time as it was for me to understand theirs. They took little interest in days and minutes and seconds. They were led by their moods and circumstances, whereas I was still controlled by my expectations.

Fortunately for Mr. Hansen, he learned a second description which allowed him to live in either reality; may the reader succeed as well.

The other point of this strange sensation is a deja vu - greeting old friends I haven't seen in years. In 1985, Judith Ann DeLozier and I developed an entirely new descriptive code for the enterprise called NLP. The material in this Manual is drawn from the old code - the classic code developed primarily by Bandler and me from 1972 - 1979. DeLozier and I argue in our new coding (Turtles All The Way Down) that if there is any wisdom and balance in human affairs it surely must reside in discovering and appreciating without reductionism multiple non-translatable descriptions of the world. This principle applies at every logical level, including NLP. Thus questions about whether the new code is better, more accurate, ... than the old code are missing the point entirely. The fact that there are now two descriptions begins to create a balance and wisdom in the endeavor.

One may be permitted to have preference - I, myself, prefer the new code in Turtles. No doubt, this is due in part to pride of authorship (with Judith DeLozier) - although I was the co-author with Bandler of the old code. I think that there may be one instructive point in my preference. The new code has few technical barriers to immediate application - whereas the old code requires a training front in which certain technical distinctions must be appreciated before one can use it. As such the new code meets an important criterion which surely must inform the behavior of any modeler. Specifically, a modeler has a responsibility to create models which are universal - that is, descriptions which any reasonably organized human can learn. After all, a modeler, by definition, makes a complex set of skills, attitudes, beliefs, ... explicit in as simple a form as is consistent with the effect to be achieved. Technical fronts and technical language (jargon) are indications of the creation of an elite - always a questionable social movement. In sum the new code is far less technical and more balanced than the old code, thus more available and universal a description.

These last remarks come, please note, from the co-author of both descriptions. I urge you to master both, for it is out of the irreducible tension between the two that some balance can occur.

With these caveats, the Manual represents a significant contribution amidst the flood of questionable and inflated recent publications and will work just in case you, the reader, act on the basis of these descriptions. Therefore, my compliments to Charlotte Bretto for her fine work.

John Grinder

FOREWORD

My path to the discipline of Neuro Linguistic Programming ™ (NLP) probably formally began in an elective course, Human Relations 303, taught at the University of Miami, Miami, Florida, by a Gestalt psychologist. Being a biology major there was a natural link for me to the Gestalt model of thinking about human behavior. My curiosity lead me to shift my major, at which time I enrolled in classes that introduced me to the work of Gregory Bateson and Milton H. Erickson.

In 1978 I had the good fortune of not receiving my first choice of a workshop session at an international conference and got my second choice of a session conducted by John T. Grinder on Neuro-Linguistic Programming. Since this first introduction 10 years ago I have gone on to apprentice with John, direct the Southeast Center of NLP (SCNLP), a division of the Center for Professional Development, and become an Associate of Grinder, DeLozier and Associates.

During my time as Director of SCNLP I frequently received requests, from students for a reference manual on this discipline whose domain is the structure of subjective experience. From looking at the bibliography it is easy to see how such a reference book could be useful to the field. The interesting challenge to me is to remember that this is a manual that will never be finished because the field keeps growing and changing, like all dynamic systems.

Since this manual began as a reference manual for Practitioner level certification in the art of NLP there are valuable concepts and tools in the field which are not included. For example, advanced work in sub-modalities, meta-programming, criteria, beliefs, sleight-of-mouth patterns, metaphor and other patterns identified through the modeling of Milton H. Erickson. For further information on these please consult the bibliography.

The task of summarizing several major conceptions, some in print and some only available on audio tape, was quite a project. Participants in the 1986-87 NLP Practitioner Program held in Raleigh, North Carolina were the first to see my initial efforts. Their enthusiasm and helpful feedback assisted me in moving forward.

Since that time my good friends Mary Boren and Barbara Moyer have held my life-line, kicked me a few times, and provided invaluable editorial feedback. Barbara, with assistance from Suzanne Bailey on design, has brought this to a finished product after hours of labor on our friendly MacIntosh. I would like to express my deepest appreciation to all those people who have encouraged me to complete this manual, to the individuals, authors and publishers who have granted permission to use material in print, and to Greg Hill for teaching me to use the MacIntosh.

Since 1978, I have acquired a full two-drawer filing cabinet of handouts and a bookcase full of books on or related to the field. Every attempt has been made to cite appropriate references and secure appropriate releases for the use of included material. If by some chance I missed something of yours or of someone you know please let me know so corrections can be made in future reprints.

My hope is that as you read you will remember that the map is not the territory and there is no substitute for feedback from the world. Kuan Tsu once said, "*What a man desires to know is that* (i.e., the external). *But his means of knowing is this* (i.e. himself). *How can he know that? Only by perfecting this.*"

INTRODUCTION

THE NLP MODEL AND "PRESUPPOSITIONS"

NLP is a model; it is not a theory nor is it concerned with ultimate truth about human behavior. These are the presuppositions upon which that model is built. To test a presupposition, act as if it were true and notice the results you get.

I.   Everyone lives in their own unique model of the world.

2.   People always make the best choices available to them, given their unique model of the world and of the situation.

'3.   There is a solution (a desirable outcome) to every problem.

4.   Everyone already has everything they need to solve all of their problems.

5.   There is a distinction between a person and the behaviors they exhibit. When someone is learning something new, it is useful to evaluate the behaviors while holding constant a positive evaluation of self.

6.   The behavior a person exhibits is separate from the intention or purpose of that behavior. The intention is always assumed to be positive.

7.   The meaning of a communication is the response it elicits. The intention behind a commmunication is not its meaning.

8.   In interactions among people, the person with the most flexibility and variation of behavior can control the outcome of the interaction. (In cybernetics this is known as the Law of Requisite Variety.)

9.   Memory and imagination use the same neurological circuits and potentially have the same impact.

10.   Knowledge, thought, memory, and imagination are the result of sequences and combinations of representational systems.

11.   Mind and body are part of the same cybernetic structure and anything that occurs in one part of the system will affect the other parts.

12.   If what you are doing isn't working, do something different.

AN INTRODUCTION TO NEURO LINGUISTIC PROGRAMMING

Neuro Linguistic Programming is the discipline whose domain is the structure of subjective experience. It makes no commitment to theory, but rather has the status of a model - a set of procedures whose usefulness is to be the measure of its worth. NLP presents specific tools which can be applied effectively in any human interaction. It offers specific techniques by which a practitioner may usefully organize and re-organize his or her subjective experience or the experiences of a client in order to define and subsequently secure any behavioral outcome.

There are three characteristics of effective patterning in NLP which sharply distinguish it from behavioral science as it is commonly practiced today. First, for a pattern or generalization regarding human communication to be acceptable or well-formed in NLP, it must include in the description the human agents who are initiating and responding to the pattern being described, their actions, and their possible responses. Second, the description of the pattern must be represented in sensorily grounded terms which are available to the user. This user-oriented constraint on NLP ensures usefulness. Since patterns must be represented in sensorily-grounded terms available to the user, a pattern will typically have multiple representations, each tailored for the differing sensory capabilities of individual users. This requirement immediately excludes statistical statements about patterning. Third, NLP includes within its descriptive vocabulary terms which are not directly observable.

At present, you have before you a written representation of the model called NLP. The term model is chosen deliberately and in contrast to the term theory. A model is simply a description of how something works without any commitment regarding why it might be that way. A theory is taxed with the task of finding justifications of why various models seem to fit reality. We are modelers and we ask that you evaluate this work as a model, ignoring whether it is true or false, correct or incorrect, aesthetically pleasing or not, in favor of discovering whether it works or not, whether it is useful or not.

Also, be reassured that what you might experience as complex or difficult in the NLP model as you absorb the written representation is an artifact of the medium in which it is represented. In our various seminars for executives, attorneys, managers, sales personnel, educators, therapists, and other professionals, the live presentation of NLP in a face-to-face context with immediate feedback has consistently resulted in a highly effective and enjoyable learning experience.

Neuro Linguistic Programming is a model about the special world of magic and illusion of human behavior and communication - the study of the components of perception and behavior which make our experience possible. The name Neuro Linguistic Programming stands for what we maintain to be the basic process used by all human beings to encode, transfer, guide, and modify behavior.

For us, behavior is programmed by combining and sequencing neural system representations - sights, sounds, feelings, smells, and tastes - whether that behavior involves making a decision, throwing a football, smiling at someone, visualizing the spelling of a word, or teaching physics. A given input stimulus is processed through a sequence of internal representations, and a specific behavioral outcome is generated.

"Neuro" (derived from the Greek, "neuron," for nerve) stands for the fundamental tenet that all behavior is the result of neurological processes. "Linguistic" (derived from the Latin, "lingua," for language) indicates that neural processes are represented, ordered, and sequenced into models and strategies through language and communication systems. "Programming" refers to the process of organizing the components of a system (sensory representations, in this case) to achieve specific outcomes.

No matter what background or occupation you have, you have probably at some time or other had the experience of interacting with someone on the stage on which you perform in a way that was particularly effective and allowed you to get some specific outcome that was of importance for you, the other person, or a number of people. This may have been the communication or learning of some important information, making a sale, solving a problem, and so on. Afterwards, though delighted with yourself, you may have had no real idea of what it was that characterized and distinguished that occasion and the effectiveness, speed, and elegance of your communication from a normal situation.

Or perhaps you have met a person or had the experience of spending time with an individual who is eminently successful in a particular field, and you have wondered what characterized the differences in their behavior from yours or from that of other individuals. You may have asked yourself what is it that allows them to do what may seem incredible or magical to others.

Or perhaps you yourself have a particular talent or ability that you would like to offer or teach to others, but have no idea of what it is that enables you to perform your task with such elegance and sophistication.

What NLP is about is how to unpack and repackage behavior, like that in the examples above, into efficient and communicable sequences that will be available to every member of the species. It will provide you with a set of tools that will enable you to analyze and incorporate or modify any sequence of behavior that you may observe in another human being.

Human beings have evolved many systems or models for understanding and dealing with the universe we live in. These models for organizing and coding the interaction of people in their environment have names such as culture, religion, art, philosophy, politics, industry, and science. Each model overlaps with other models and may include smaller models nested inside itself, just as science includes physics, biology, oceanography, chemistry, etc., and overlaps with industry in areas of research. Each model differs from the others in the portion of human experience it represents and emphasizes and in the way it organizes and uses its selected set of representations. All are similar in their ultimate concern with the outcomes of human behavior.

The purpose of each model is to identify patterns in the interaction between human behavior and the environment so that the behavior of individual human beings can be systematized within the selected context to achieve desired outcomes more efficiently, effectively, and consistently. For example, scientists are trained to operate within a specific model to help them organize their behavioral priorities in gathering and interpreting data. They are taught to recognize and work toward specific desired outcomes, as are business people, artists, politicians, and medical doctors.

As participant organisms within the universe, we, the model-makers who devise, perpetuate, and extend our cultural models, do not operate directly on the world. Rather, we operate through coded interpretations of the environment as received and experienced through our sensory representational systems - through sight, sound, smell, taste, and feeling. Information about our external universe (as well as our internal states) is received, organized, consolidated, and transmitted through an internal system of neural pathways that culminate in the brain - our central processing biocomputer. This information is then transformed through internal processing strategies that each individual has learned. The result is what we call "behavior." In NLP behavior is defined as all sensory representations experienced and expressed internally and/or externally for which evidence is available from a subject and/or from a human observer of that subject. That is, the act of skiing down a beautiful snow-covered mountainside and the act of imagining oneself doing so are equally to be considered behaviors in the context of NLP.

Both macro-behavior and micro-behavior are, of course, programmed through our neurological systems. Macro-behavior is overt and easily observable, as in driving a car, speaking, fighting, eating, getting sick, or riding a bicycle. Micro-behavior involves subtler though equally important phenomena such as heart rate, voice tempo, skin color changes, pupil dilation and such events as seeing in the mind's eye or having an internal dialogue.

Obviously not all culturally transmitted models for behavior have been incorporated into all members of the human species, but most of us have many of them available in our representational systems. The development, then, of these models - and the behavior generated through them - form a significant statement about the neurological systems of those individuals who have adopted them as organizational strategies for their behavior. That is, the variety and range of human behavior, viewed in the context of the models that generate those behaviors, tells us much about human neurological organization. The state of these models today - the most current point in their development - represents the evolution of ideas, the surviving wisdom of our predecessors. Ultimately, after the uproar of economic, religious, and ideological disputes has subsided, models are kept or discarded on the basis of their adaptiveness or usefulness as guides for the behavior of members of the species. The acceptance or rejection, elaboration and expansion of these models reflects the evolution of human thought and behavior.

Neuro Linguistic Programming is a natural extension of this evolutionary process - a new model. It is important to realize that models such as those described above are not simply "out there" somewhere, external to us as individuals. Rather, politics, religion, psychology and the other models are ways of looking at, talking about, and feeling about the same experiential domain: human behavior. NLP differs from other models of behavior in that it is specifically a model of our behavior as model makers. It is what we call a meta-model, a model of the modeling process itself.

Implicit in NLP as a meta-model is its broad range of practical application. From individual interactions to group, corporate and system dynamics of any kind, the behavioral parameters can be identified, organized, and programmed to obtain specific objectives. When the confusions and complexities of life experience are examined, sorted, and untangled what remains is a set of behavioral elements and rules that aren't so difficult to understand after all. In this certification training program, we will describe techniques and applications derived from NLP and designed for use in behavioral interactions in any area of human endeavor.

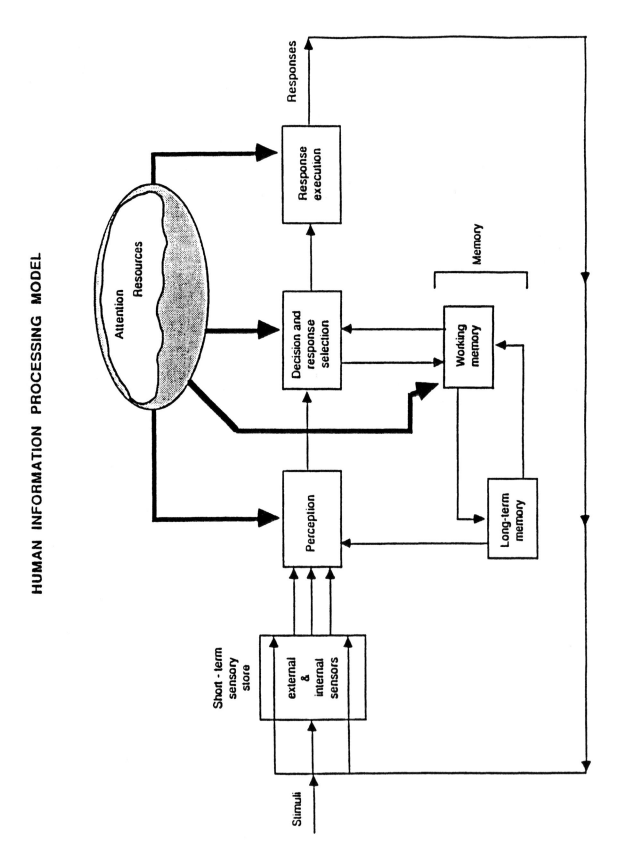

HUMAN INFORMATION PROCESSING MODEL

HUMAN INFORMATION PROCESSING MODEL

The model depicted on the previous page is a useful simplifying framework for interpreting human performance in complex tasks. However, it is important to realize that it is simplified, and that not all aspects of the representation should be taken literally. In particular, three important qualifications should be highlighted.

First, the "flow" of information has been portrayed in the previous diagram as moving from initial reception to response execution. There are many instances, however, in which the processes operate in reverse order, particularly in cases where our interpretation of sensory data is greatly influenced by our *expectancies*, generated from short- and long-term memory as well as by the outcome of our previous decisions. Bobrow and Norman (1975) have referred to the distinction between "data-driven," or "bottom up," processes (those operating left to right in the diagram) and "conceptually driven," or "top down," processes. Decisions that have already been made or information already stored in memory may influence the perceptual categorizations made.

Second, these operations, or stages, should not be thought of as literal boxes or even necessarily as physical locations within the brain. Rather, they represent functional transformations performed on the information as it is processed. It may be that some of the mental operations can, in fact, be structurally localized to particular regions or physical networks within the brain. Definable areas in the cortex, for example, seem to be responsible for early stages of sensory and perceptual analysis. Yet in most instances, correlations between information-processing paradigms and physiological manifestations of brain activity are still too sparse to make definitive localization possible.

Third, the distinction between processing stages may not be as clear as indicated, although there do appear to be both logical and experimental grounds for distinguishing between the three processes of perception, action selection, and response execution. More importantly, although the diagram suggests a discreet temporal sequencing (i.e., perception is terminated before response selection begins), this sequencing may not be absolute. In fact, recent research suggests that information is not handed along stage by stage like a car on an assembly line. Rather, it undergoes a continuous "flow," with considerable overlap in time between the operation of different processing stages (Eriksen & Schultz, 1978; McClelland, 1979). For example, the response selection process may begin for a particular stimulus even before that stimulus has been absolutely and categorically recognized.

Sensory processing: Of primary importance in engineering psychology are the visual and auditory senses of the eyes, ears, and the proprioceptive or kinesthetic senses of body and limb position. Unique limitations on each sensory system influence the quality and quantity of information that may be initially registered and so, potentially, all processes that follow. The characteristics of rod and cone receptors in the retina of the eye, for example, influence the conditions under which color can be employed to display information.

Short-term sensory store: Each sensory system, or *modality*, appears to be equipped with a central mechanism that prolongs a representation of the physical stimulus for a short period of time after the stimulus has physically terminated. When attention is diverted elsewhere, the short-term sensory store (STSS) permits environmental information to be preserved temporarily and dealt with later. Three general properties are characteristic of STSS:

1. It is *preattentive*; that is, no conscious attention is required to prolong the image during the natural "time constant" of the store.

2. It is relatively *veridical*, preserving most of the physical details of the stimulus.

3. It is *rapidly decaying*. The particular time constant of the decay varies somewhat, normally being less than a second for short-term visual store (STVS or iconic memory; Neisser, 1967; Sperling, 1960) and a bit longer for both short-term kinesthetic and auditory store (Posner & Konick, 1966). Estimates for the last two range between 2 and 8 seconds, depending upon the techniques employed in measurement (Lackman, Lachman, and Butterfield, 1979).

Perceptual encoding: STSS preserves the details of the stimulus image only briefly and without attention . The information is then processed by progressively higher contact with a unique neural code that was previously *learned* and *stored* in the brain. At this point the stimulus is said to be preceived or recognized. The result is a *perceptual decision* in which the physical stimulus is assigned to a single perceptual category. The effect on perception of the previously learned neural code is represented in the diagram by the association between perception and *Long-term memory*, the repository of relatively permanent information. The perceptual process is a many-to-one mapping; that is, a large number of different physical stimuli may be assigned to a single perceptual category. For example, in perception of the letter a, different type styles (A, a, or *a*) all generate the same categorical perception, as does the sound "a" spoken by any voice. At the same time that there is a common response to all these forms of the letter a, their differences are also preserved at higher levels of processing. Mechanisms of focal attention allow us, if we choose, to attend to other dimensions of the stimulus as well, such as whether it is spoken by a male or female voice, or written in upper or lower case. Even with this flexibility, however, the common response to the various physical forms of "a" will remain.

In more complex tasks, at least two dimensions must be considered to match a particular stimulus category. Such multidimensional considerations typify the task of *pattern recognition*. Each pattern is uniquely specified by a combination of levels (called features) along the several physical dimensions. For instance, recognition of a particular malfunction of a complex system will occur when the operator can associate a unique combination (pattern) of dial readings (features) on several different instruments (dimensions) to the perceptual category associated with a particular malfunctioning state. Pattern recognition of a disease by a physician is elicited by certain unique combinations of features called symptoms. A particular collection of thermometer and barometer readings, satellite cloud-cover photos, and wind speeds may signal "storm coming" to a trained meterorologist. Pattern recognition of a "state" by an NLP practitioner is elicited by certain unique combinations of features called verbal and nonverbal behaviors through a technique called calibration.

Decision-Making: Once a stimulus has been perceptually categorized, the operator must decide what to do with it. For example, recognizing that a traffic light has turned yellow (an absolute judgement task), the driver may decide to accelerate or to brake. In this case, the decision involves the selection of a response. Alternatively, as indicated in the diagram, the driver may decide to store the information in memory while searching the intersection ahead for the presence of a police car. If the decision is made to commit the information to memory, then the information flow in the diagram follows the path leading to the memory box. At this point, a second decision may be made to retain the information for a short time by actively rehearsing it in "working memory" or attempting to store it permanently (learn it) and so enter the information in long-term memory. It is apparent that the point of decision-making and response selection is a critical junction in the sequence of information processing. A large degree of choice is involved, and heavy potential costs and benefits depend upon the correctness of the decision.

Response execution: If a decision is made to generate a response, then an added series of steps is required to call up, and release with the appropriate timing and force, the necessary muscle commands to carry out the action. The decision to initiate the response is logically separate from its execution. The baseball batter, for example, may decide to swing or not swing at a pitch (response selection) and, if he does swing, may execute one of a variety of successful or unsuccessful swings of the bat (response execution).

Feedback: It is evident that we typically monitor the consequences of our actions, forming the closed-loop feedback structure depicted in the diagram. While feedback most often is considered in terms of a visual feedback loop (i.e., we see the consequences of our responses), feedback through the auditory, proprioceptive, and tactile (skin senses) modalities may be at least as important under some circumstances. For example, when changing gears in an automobile, the proprioceptive feedback from the hand is of considerable importance in evaluating when the gears have been engaged successfully.

Attention: Much of the processing that occurs following STSS appears to require attention to function efficiently. In this context, we may model attention both as a searchlight that chooses information sources to process and as a commodity or *resource* of limited availability. If some processes require more of this resource, then less is available for other processes, whose performance therefore will deteriorate. We need only note how one stops talking in a car (response selection and execution) if there is a sudden need to scan a crowded freeway for a critical road sign (perception). Yet learning and practice decrease the demand for the limited supply of resources. We can walk while talking because walking, a well-practiced skill, requires little attention.

THE NLP PROCESS

The goal of Neuro Linguistic Programming (NLP) is to integrate the macroscopic information about human behavior and experience available to each of us through our sensory experience with the unobservable microscopic information of the neuro physiology of behavior and experience into a useful cybernetic model. I believe such an integration is essential if we ever hope to understand or utilize the properties governing the complex human processes of learning, memory, communication, choice, and motivation and how these affect the social and ecological environments of human beings.

NLP was founded by behavioral modelers John Grinder and Richard Bandler to analyze and explore the patterns governing such complex processes of human behavior. The basic premise of NLP is that there is a redundancy between the observable macroscopic patterns of human behavior (for example, linguistic and paralinguistic phenomena, eye movements, hand and body position, and other types of performance distinctions) and patterns of the underlying neural activity governing this behavior.

For example, we have probably all noticed in the course of some conversation, another individual, in response to some question, slow down the tempo of his/her voice while trying to recall the requested information, then suddenly flick his/her eyes up and to the left, breaking perceptual contact momentarily. This movement is generally followed by an increase in tempo as the individual describes or talks about some object or event, usually using language indicative of some sort of visual representation. One might say that this behavior is indicative of the access of some internal visual image (that is, activity in the visual cortex of the brain separate from the visual information being provided by the individual's immediate sensory experience).

Similarly, if one observes another individual or that same individual orient his/her head down and to the left in response to some question, put a hand over his/her mouth, and mutter "hmmmmm," eventually responding with some utterance describing what that individual has heard about some object or event, one might conclude that this segment of behavior is indicative of some neural process that is qualitatively different from that indicated by the behavioral segment previously described. If one can determine the correlation between these segments and the individual's internal experience and patterns (consistency and combinations) involving their use, one might be able to make assumptions and predictions concerning the personality and behavior of another individual and act on this knowledge.

The previous two examples are simple and relatively meaningless when presented in the absence of other contextual information concerning the entire communication sequence. And, indeed, Neuro Linguistic Programming involves an examination of the entire system of feedback and response, both behaviorally and biologically, occuring in the interactions between (a) a human being and him/herself, (b) a human being and other human beings, and (c) a human being and his/her environment.

Neuro Linguistic Programming is a process and at the same time a model of a process (as are most scientific and cybernetic models). All of the information, laws, patterns, and conclusions made by the model about past experience are only important or useful in the way that they relate to one's immediate ongoing experience. This is especially important to keep in mind when one is dealing with another cybernetic system (in this case, a human being) that is subject to many levels of change, depending on its interactions with itself, its social environment and its ecological environment.

A basic outline of the Neuro Linguistic Programming process:

A. **Train and expand one's own sensory awareness of other human beings to:**

    1.   Observe and identify meaningful patterns of behavior which are systematic, recurring, and a part of everyone's sensory experience.

    2.   Notice what responses one's own choice of behavior elicits in oneself and other human beings (and vice versa).

B. **Utilize the information one gathers through these observations to determine:**

    1.   The representational distinctions human beings can make about their internal and external experience, i.e., their ability to see/visualize, hear/verbalize, etc.

2. Patterns involving the combination and connections of neural networks (sensory representation) underlying behavioral processes.

3. How these distinctions and patterns affect the strategies people use to organize, make sense of, and communicate about their sensory experience and internal maps.

4. How these distinctions, patterns and strategies may be utilized to understand and promote the processes of, among other things, learning, communication, motivation, and choice in human beings within the individual and his/her social and ecological environments.

The **mechanics of this process** may be generalized into the following basic procedure:

a. An outcome is identified that is mutually acceptable to the facilitator (programmer) and the client (programmee). Explicit criteria for the successful achievement of the outcome are delineated.

b. One individual (the programmer) generates a communication, in the form of verbal and non-verbal behavior, in an attempt to direct or propel the programmee to the desired outcome. This communication elicits a response in the form of some access of information and return communication on the part of the other individual, the programmee. The interaction will take place on both the verbal and nonverbal level of response.

c. The two individuals may then work together to make distinctions in the programmee's experience and response, both internally and externally:

    1. via the programmer's perception of the programmee's external behavior within the specific contextual setting.

    2. via explicit discussion and questioning about the programmee's internal experience.

d. The distinctions may then be classified and segmented into a formula that traces the programmee's behavior in terms of relevant input, mental processing and behavioral output.

e. The information provided by these patterns and distinctions is utilized to make decisions and predictions about the individual's current and future behavior, and to devise more effective strategies the programmee can use to achieve desired outcomes.

f. The programmer then varies his/her behavior in accordance with this information, and the process repeats itself until the outcome is reached.

THE PROBLEMS OF LIFE;
BERTALANFFY AND GENERAL SYSTEMS THEORY

Ludwig von Bertalanffy was a Viennese professor of biology who emigrated to Canada in 1949. Soon afterwards he founded the Society for the Advancement of General Systems Theory and remains its acknowledged inspiration; he had been nominated for a Nobel Prize when he died in 1971. His book, Problems of Life, is a classic treatise on the failure of 'robotic' and reductive explanations of living organisms. When, he asked, does a live sponge reduced to mush by being forced through a fine sieve spontaneously reorganize itself? Why, when certain 'organizer' cells are transplanted from the leg to the tail of an embryo newt, does the creature grow two tails? How do you explain 'equifinality', that when an organism's usual path to its end state of development is blocked it will take path after path, repeatedly, to achieve that end, such that when organs usually employed in this process are damaged, as in injury to sections of the brain, other parts will come into play to replace them.

Bertalanffy's answer to these observations, given thirty years before such models gained acceptance, was that life is first and foremost a system of self-organization, a developmental unfolding at progressively higher levels of differentiation and organized complexity. These wholes are not reducible to their parts and their developed forms are qualitatively different from earlier forms. The organism, moreover, is dynamic rather than static, open not closed, and searches spontaneously and actively for stimulation, rather than waiting passively to respond. However Bertalanffy was not content to remain with biology. If the organism was an open system interacting with its environment, could biology as a discipline do anything less? He joked about psychologists who claimed that their discipline was at a crossroads. Psychology *is* a crossroads and the mind a meeting-point for symbolic systems. From this conviction general systems thoery was founded, aided by the converging efforts of such persons as Norman Weiner in cybernetics, Anatol Rapoport in game theory, Heinz Werner in psychology, and Claude Shannon in communications.

General systems theory is thus a 'discipline of disciplines' with special emphases on psychobiology and ecology. It is a study of those wholes whose principles are comparable whatever the nature of their particular components. For example, the cybernetic feedback model came originally from the technology of thermostats and govenors on steam engines, but it has considerable validity for social, personality and value systems generally. But to take the simplest example first, the map shows the minimum necessary components of a cybernetic system.

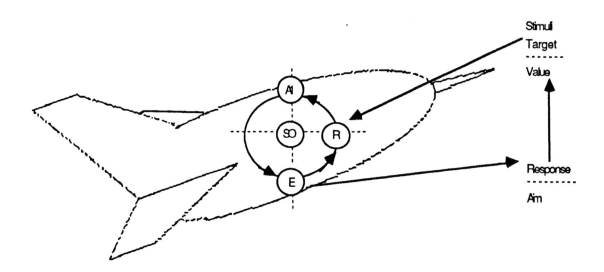

Stimuli register upon a receptor, R, which scans specifically for them. From R, information codes (not the thing itself) travel to the direction center, A1, which by amplifying, inhibiting or otherwise steering the system triggers action in the effector, E. From here two kinds of messages flow: one sends a response which may effect the stimuli, the other is a feedback loop to the receptor which informs it of the action taken by the effector. This completes the self-correcting system. In the case of a heat-seeking guided missile, the effector would inform the receptor that direction changes had been made to track a shifting target.

To convert this system to the condition of a live organism it is necessary to add a self-organizing capacity (SO). This would include the genetic code which instructs the organism to develop. In humans it would also involve the various capacities of mind - the purposive feedforward devices of the holographic memory store, varieties of creative bisociation, sequentially unfolding stages of moral judgment and a grammar of linguistically generated values. It is such characteristics of human mind that turn targets into values and mere responses into ethical aims. Thus to transcend hostile academic disciplines and warring international systems, we must develop self-organizing general systems of symbolic relationships which reconcile empiricism with dialectics, classes and races, and the human species with its environments.

"Warren [Warren S. McCulloch, 1898-1969] was speaking very slowly. I am by nature a warrior and wars don't make sense any more. I am a king, but I'm an anarchist, and in my country there are simply no laws. . .Now the difficulty is that we, who are not single-celled organisms, cannot simply divide and pass on our programs. We have to couple and there is behind this a second requirement. Warren began to weep. We learn. . .that there's a utility in death because. . .the world goes on changing and we can't keep up with it. If I have any disciples, you can say this of every one of them, they think for themselves."

"Very softly Gregory said, 'Sure Warren.'

"Freedom from and freedom for. We sat in silence for a long pause. 'Coffee?' said Warren."

From the 'Conference on the Effects of Conscious Purpose on Human Adaptation' July, 1969, convened by Gregory Bateson, quoted by Catherine Bateson in Our Own Metaphor .

ECOLOGICAL SYSTEMS APPROACH

Ecology: 1.   The branch of biology that deals with the relations between living organisms and their environment.

                  2.   In sociology, the relationship between the distribution of human groups with reference to material resources and the consequent social and cultural patterns.

Ecological: of or by ecology.

This approach advocates the realignment of current knowledge and re-examination of human behavior within a holistic model, that of ecological phenomenology. It is aimed at constructing a model for a unified science. The Systems Approach is a way of thinking and an operational style. The vantage point of the data collectors focuses precisely on the interfaces and communication processes taking place. It begins with an analysis of the structure of the field, using the common structural and operational properties of systems as criteria for identifying the systems and subsystems within.

The common **structural and operational properties of a system** (criteria for identification of systems and subsystems):

        1.   Organization

        2.   Integration

        3.   Interaction

        4.   Interdependency

        5.   Structure

        6.   Stability

By tracing the communication within and between systems, the systems approach insists that the structure, sources, pathways, repository sites, and integrative functions of messages become clear in addition to their content. (Bateson, 1950) This approach is based on the communication concept of behavior first described by Gregory Bateson in California in the 1950's.

General basis of Communication Theory:

1. All behavior is communicative - even refusal to speak is a comment on the relationship of those involved in the communication.

2. Messages have report and command aspects. "It is raining", is a report message and, depending on the context and relationship between listener and sharer, it may be a command to, "Remember your umbrella."

3. Command messages define the relationship - this is the troublesome part. They are the medium through which relationships are shaped and in this process ambiguity, misunderstanding and duplicity are possible. Often communicants are unaware of commands they are giving, receiving, and/or obeying.

4. Families' and groups' command messages are patterned as rules. Two or more people in relationship for a long time exchange commands which assume patterns from which rules for the relationship may be derived. These constrain and order the behavior of family/group members in patterns of mutual influence that have cybernetic properties.

5. Change and stability - If a family/group/individual wants to change the relationship, the regulation response of others (or other functions of self) which stabilize the system by reducing change makes it appear that the conservative element in the system resides in the person (function) attempting to change it.

6. Inability to change rules is system pathology. A system is considered pathological when the rules are set in such a way that there is no way of changing them. This happens when two rules paradoxically negate each other: e.g., "Mother decides when we go to bed"; and "None of us believe that anyone sets the rule for bedtime - we all need sleep for our health". In such a family it is impossible to negotiate about bedtime without breaking one or both of the rules.

7. The communication specialist must install him/herself as the meta-communicator or change-maker of the family/group/functions of self. He/she helps the family/group/function to get unstuck. The general form of the process is that he/she is the third person/function to whom two or more others/functions present themselves with their "stuck," endlessly cycling system. He/she intervenes to change the rules because they can not.

LOGICAL LEVELS AND CHUNKING INFORMATION

An interesting theoretical structure for understanding the kinds of learnings available to human beings evolved from Bertrand Russell's theory of Logical Types and was described in 1964 by Gregory Bateson, in his article, "The Logical Categories of Learning and Communication", in <u>Steps to an Ecology of Mind.</u>

In that article, Bateson describes his view that learning takes place on different **logical levels** - learning, learning to learn, etc., such that a given level of learning (above zero learning) has below it another level which includes learning subsets of the level above. On one level, I learn how to do all the kinds of procedures included in addition, multiplication and subtraction, without understanding how they work. On the next level, I learn how these calculations work, in a way that allows me to proceed on my own to learn how, for example, to do division. Learning on the next level would, then, allow me to understand how I learned how to do those calculations. This is derived from Russell's theory that "a class of classes cannot be one of the classes which are its members; that a name is not the thing named." The name of an object is at a logical level higher than, or "meta" to, the object. In Bateson's theory, each learning level is meta to - encompasses, names, or describes - the elements of the set of learnings below it. <u>Cybernetically, moving from one learning level up to the next allows a person to have more "requisite variety" - a cybernetic term which means, in this context, more actual survival strength through greater flexibility in an organism's ability to cope with the variety of situations found in a lifetime.</u>

Within practitioner training we are interested in you gaining the ability to "switch" logical levels when coding and recoding information. This skill can be used to determine outcomes, to handle objections externally and/or internally, and to change perceptual filters (see things differently).

Chunking is our word for shifting logical levels in a communication. Sometimes it's useful to shift from focusing on the "Big Picture" to the detail, from the general to the specific. Sometimes it's useful to shift in the other direction. **Milton Model Language Patterns** are very "large chunks" (i.e., unspecified verbs, nominalizations, etc.) allowing the client to sort through many different experiences and representations and choose from them in order to make sense of the communication. **Meta-Model Challenges** take non-specific communications and force the subject to be more specific, to move in the direction of description at the sensory level, "smaller chunks" (i.e., what specifically, how specifically, etc.). **Metaphor Construction** takes information in a specific communication and generates communication similar in structure and different in content, "sideways chunks" (e.g.,talking about a single parent and two children via a gardener and two rose bushes).

In terms of human behavior: chunking up combines parts of experience or behavior into larger groups or categories, (e.g., moving to a new apartment - asking, What will that do for you?). Chunking down breaks the experience in behavior down to its component parts (e.g., representational systems and submodalities). Chunking Sideways (laterally) creates behavioral alternatives, like sidestepping, (e.g., anxious behavior is not okay when talking to old friends and is okay when talking to a group for the first time).

For **chunking up,** ask yourself:	"What is this an example of?"
For **chunking down,** ask yourself:	"What is an example or component of this?"
For **chunking sideways,** ask yourself:	"What is another example of the same class?"

For example:

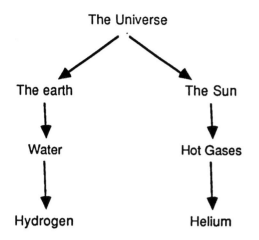

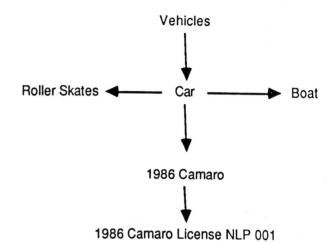

REPRESENTATIONAL SYSTEMS

REPRESENTATIONAL SYSTEMS:
THE BUILDING BLOCKS OF BEHAVIOR

The basic elements from which the patterns of human behavior are formed are the perceptual systems through which the members of the species operate on their environment: **vision** (sight), **audition** (hearing), **kinaesthesis** (body sensations), and **olfaction /gustation** (smell/taste). The NLP model presupposes that all of the distinctions we human beings are able to make concerning our environment (internal and external) and our behavior can be usefully represented in terms of these systems. These perceptual classes constitute the structural parameters of human knowledge.

We postulate that all of our ongoing experience can be usefully coded as consisting of some combination of these sensory classes. In our previous work (see Grinder, et. al., Patterns II) we chose to represent and abbreviate the expresson of on-going sensory experience as a 4-tuple. The 4-tuple is shown symbolically as:

$$<A(e,i), V(e,i), K(e,i), O(e,i)>$$

Here the capital letters are abbreviations for the major sensory classes or representational systems:

A = Auditory/Hearing
V = Visual/Sight
K = Kinesthetic/Body Sensations
O = Olfactory/Gustatory - Smell/Taste

The superscripts (in parentheses) "e" and "i" indicate whether the representations are coming from sources external, to us ("e"), as when we are looking at, listening to, feeling, smelling or tasting something that is outside of us, or whether they are internally generated, ("i"), as when we are remembering or imagining some image, sound, feeling, smell or taste. We can also show the 4-tuple iconically as:

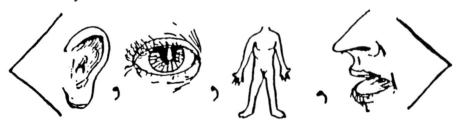

The following excerpt from <u>Patterns II</u> will further assist you in understanding the 4-tuple:

"Assuming that you are a reader who at this point in time is sitting comfortably in a quiet place and that you are reading alone, the 4-tuple can be used to represent your present experience of the world as follows: where "i" is the referential index of the reader and the blank space "0" indicates no experience in that mode.

the printed words of the book, the lighting pattern of the room . . .	the feeling of the chair, the temperature of the room . . .	0	the smell of the room, the freshness of the air . . .

"In words, the reader's present experience of the world is represented by a description of the visual input from the words, his present kinesthetic sensations and the olfactory sensation available. Since, by our assumption, the reader is in a place where he is presently receiving no auditory input from the external world, the value of the variable $A(t)$ (the auditory tonal portion of his experience) is 0. The values of the V, K and O variables are specified by a description of the input from the world that is impinging on the reader at this point in time. Notice that in specifying the 4-tuple for the reader's present experience, we restricted ourselves to representing experience originating in the world external to the reader. The 4-tuple can also be used to represent the reader's total experience - that is his present ongoing experience independently of whether it originates in the world external to the reader or not. We have found it useful in our work to identify the origin of the portion of the experience described in the 4-tuple - that is to distinguish between which portion of the experience represented by the 4-tuple originates in the world external to the person whose experience is represented by the 4-tuple and which portion is generated by the person's own internal processes. One easy way of representing this distinction is by simply attaching a superscript to each component of the 4-tuple - either an i (internally generated) or an e (externally generated). Thus assuming that the reader is reading with internal dialogue at this point in time and using the superscripts which distinguish the internally generated from externally originated components of the 4-tuple, the reader's 4-tuple would look like:

the printed words of the book, the lighting pattern in the room . . .e	the feeling of the chair, the temperature of the room . . . e	the tempo and tonal qualities of the reader's internal dialogue. . i	the smell of the room, the freshness of the air . . .e

"As with all the distinctions in the model, this superscript distinction between internally and externally generated experience will be employed only when it is useful for the task for which it is to be used."

In NLP sensory systems have much more functional significance than is attributed to them by classical models in which the senses are regarded as passive input mechanisms. The sensory information or distinctions received through each of these systems initiate and/or modulate, via neural interconnections, an individual's behavioral processes and output. Each perceptual class forms a sensory-motor complex that becomes "responseable" for certain classes of behavior. These sensory-motor complexes are called **representational systems** in NLP.

Each representational system forms a three part network:

1. The first stage, **input**, involves gathering information and getting feedback from the environment (both internal and external).

2. **Representation/Processing** includes the mapping of the environment and the establishment of behavioral strategies such as learning, decision-making, information storage, etc.

3. **Output** is the casual transform of the representational mapping process.

"Behavior" in NLP refers to activity within any representational system complex at any of these stages. The acts of seeing, listening or feeling are behavior. So is "thinking" which, if broken down to its constituent parts, would include sensory specific processes like seeing in the mind's eye, listening to the internal dialogue, having feelings about something, and so on. All output, of course, is behavior - ranging from micro-behavioral outputs such as lateral eye movements, tonal shifts in the voice and breathing rates, to macro-behavioral outputs such as arguing, disease and kicking a football.

Our representational systems form the structural elements of our own behavioral models. The behavioral "vocabulary" of human beings consists of all the experiential content generated, either internally or from external sources, through the sensory channels during our lives. The maps or models that we use to guide our behavior are developed from the ordering of this experience into patterned sequences or "behavioral phrases," so to speak. The formal patterns of these sequences of representations are called **strategies** in NLP.

The way we sequence representations through our strategies will dictate the significance that a particular representation will have in our behavor, just as the sequencing of words in a sentence will determine the meaning of particular words. A specific representation in itself is relatively meaningless. What is important is how that representation functions in the context of a strategy in an individual's behavior.

Imagine a young man wearing a white smock, sitting in a comfortable position, sunlight streaming through a high window to his right and behind him. To his left is a red book with silver lettering on its cover. As we look closer, we see him staring at a large white sheet of paper, the pupils of his eyes dilated, his facial muscles slack and unmoving, his shoulder muscles slightly tense while the rest of his body is at rest. His breathing shallow, high in his chest and regular. Who is this person?

From the description he could be a physicist, visualizing a series of complex mathematical expressions which describe the physical phenomena he wishes to understand. Equally consistent with the description, the young man could be an artist, creating vivid visual fantasies in preparation for executing an oil painting. Or, the man could be a schizophrenic, consumed in a world of inner imagery so completely that he has lost his connection with the outside world.

What links these three men is that each is employing the same representational system - attending to internal visual images. What distinguishes them from one another is how each utilizes his rich inner experience of imagery. The physicist may in a moment look up to a fellow scientist and translate his images into words, communicating through his colleague's auditory system some new pattern he's discovered through his visualizations. The artist may in a moment seize the white sheet of paper and begin to rough in shapes and colors with a brush - many of them drawn directly from his inner imagery - translating inner experience into external experience. The schizophrenic may continue his internal visual reverie with such complete absorption that the images he creates within will distract him from responding to sensory information arriving from the outside world.

The physicist and the artist differ from the schizophrenic in terms of the function of their visualizations in the context of the sequence of representational system activities that affect the outcome of their behavior: in how their visualizations are utilized. The physicist and the artist can choose to attend visually to the world outside or to their own inner visual experience. The process of creating inner visual experience is the same, neurologically, for all three men. A visual representation in itself may serve as a limitation or a resource to human potential depending on how it fits into context and how it is used. The physicist and the artist control the process; the process controls the schizophrenic. For the physicist and the artist, the natural phenomenon of visualization belongs to the class of decision variables; for the schizophrenic it belongs to the class of environmental variables.

Each of you reading this sentence has a strategy for taking the peculiar patterns of black ink on this white page and making meaning out of them for yourself. These sequences of letters, like the other visualization phenomenon just described, are meaningless outside of the sensory experiences from your own personal history that you apply to them. Words, both written and spoken, are simply codes that trigger primary sensory representations in us. A word that we have never seen or heard before will have no meaning to us because we have no sensory experience to apply to it. (For a further discussion of language as secondary experience see Patterns II.)

As you read these words you may, for example, be hearing your own voice inside your head saying the words as your eye reports the visual patterns formed by letters in this sentence. Perhaps you are remembering words that someone else has spoken to you before that sounded similar to those printed here. Perhaps these visual patterns have accessed some feelings of delight or recognition within you. You may have noticed, when you first read the description of the young man in the white smock, that you made images of what you were reading - you were using the same representational strategy for making meaning that the young man in our description was using.

The ability to transform printed symbols into internal images, into auditory representations, into feelings, tastes or smells, allow us to use strategies for making meaning that are available to each of us as human beings. Certain strategies are highly effective for creating meaning in certain contexts while others are more effective for other tasks. The strategy of taking external dialogue would not be appropriate if you were listening to a record, doing therapy or playing football.

NLP Vol. 1 (Dilts, 1980) presents what are called **meta-strategies**: strategies about strategies. More specifically, this book describes how to elicit, identify, utilize, design and install strategies that allow us to operate within and upon our environment. NLP is an explicit meta-strategy designed for you - to shift dimensions of your experience from environmental variables to decision variables and, when appropriate, to assist others to do so. NLP is an explicit meta-strategy by means of which you may gain control over portions of your experience which you desire to control, an explicit meta-strategy for you to use to create choices that you presently don't have and to assist others in securing the choices they need or want.

The principles of NLP are equally applicable in assisting business executives to reorganize their priorities and generate new options; in helping scientists and engineers get the most from their research and upgrade their teaching ability; in showing educators new and remarkably effective educational system design principles; in extending to lawyers and judges features of communication that greatly facilitate settlements; in aiding therapists to more effectively and quickly aid their clients. NLP is for people interested in getting things done and enjoying themselves in the process.

An important aspect of NLP is its versatility. Its methods of pattern identification and sequencing may be generalized from individual human beings to larger order systems, from contexts involving remedial change (problem solving) to those involving evolutionary change (extending the domain of decision variables beyond the present state for an individual or system now functioning effectively). NLP may be applied as profitably to the internal organization of a bureaucratic hierarchy as to the representational systems of an individual. In all cases the formal sequencing and scheduling of activity between the structural components of a system will determine the possible outcomes of that system and the effectiveness of that system in securing those outcomes.

In an organization, its departments or employees take the place of representational systems within a single human being. Each is responsible for a certain set of inputs, processing and outputs that contribute to one or more other sets of inputs, processing and outputs of the other members of the system and of that system as a whole. By understanding the functional characteristics of the components (employees, departments, sections, divisions, etc.) of an organization, the programmer can assist in sequencing or resequencing the interactions between components to achieve the desired outcome in the most elegant and effective manner.

NLP NOTATION

REPRESENTATIONAL SYSTEMS SUPERSCRIPTS SUBSCRIPTS

A = Auditory

V = Visual

K = Kinesthetic

O = Olfactory/Gustatory

^{r} = remembered

^{c} = constructed

^{i} = internal

^{e} = external

$_t$ = tonal/tempo

$_d$ = digital (verbal)

Examples:

A^e = Auditory External

A^i = Auditory Internal

A^r = Auditory Remembered

A^c = Auditory Constructed

A^r_t = Remembered Tonal Experience

A^i_d = Internal Dialogue

V^c = Visual Constructed

K^r = Remembered Feelings

V^i = Visual Internal

K^e = Tactile Feelings

SYNESTHESIA

The existence of the ordered sequences of representation that we call strategies presupposes interconnected networks of activity at the neurological level. Crossover connections between representational system complexes, such that the activity in one representational system initiates activity in another system, is called synesthesia in NLP. Another way to say this is: Synesthesia is the term we use to describe the experience that occurs when activity in one representational system triggers activity in another.

Hearing a harsh tone of voice and feeling uncomfortable is an example of auditory-kinesthetic synesthesia. Seeing blood and feeling nauseous would be a visual-kinesthetic synesthesia. Feeling angry and blaming someone verbally inside your head would be kinesthetic-auditory synesthesia. Hearing music and imagining a beautiful scene would constitute an auditory-visual synesthesia.

Synesthesia patterns constitute a large portion of the human meaning-making process. Correlations between representational system activities are at the root of such complex processes as knowledge, choice and communication. The skills and abilities that humans develop are the direct result of the establishment of crossover connections between neural representational complexes. The major differences among individuals possessing different skills, talents and abilities are derived from the synesthesia correlations within their particular domains of experience.

By making these correlative patterns explicit, Neuro Linguistic Programming provides a working model, an applied technology for the strategic utilization of correlative patterns to secure any behavioral outcome. By identifying synesthetic sequences that lead to specific outcomes and by making them available to those who desire to achieve those outcomes we can, in essence, replicate any behavior - whether that of a businessman, scientist, healer, athlete, musician, or anyone who does something well. With the tools provided by NLP, we believe anyone can be transformed into a modern "renaissance" person.

Synesthesia - Input/Storage/Retrieval Memory

	V_i	A_i	K_i
V_e	$V_e V_i$	$V_e A_i$	$V_e K_i$
A_e	$A_e V_i$	$A_e A_i$	$A_e K_i$
K_e	$K_e V_i$	$K_e A_i$	$K_e K_i$

REPRESENTATIONAL SYSTEMS FLEXIBILITY

Purpose: To instruct you in the development of a representational system that you would like to enhance beyond your present limited use.

I. Development of Visualization Ability

a. Sit comfortably and go inside.

b. Remember a pleasant experience and begin by talking to yourself about it. As you develop this memory, add some of the non-word sounds that went with the experience. If you were at the beach, listen to the sound of waves superimposed onto your conversation. Add the background sounds to your image.

c. As you hear the sounds, pretend what the source of those sounds might look like. For waves, see a picture of waves you have seen before. If the imagined picture is hard to get, make it into a snapshot versus a movie. Play with doing it in color or black & white. Put the picture on a movie screen or in a picture frame. Add detail or make the picture include only the source of the sounds. Experiment with adding or subtracting visual submodalities. There is a combination which will make it easier for you to get a picture.

d. Once you have the start of a picture, let it develop by adding more elements.

e. Experiment by adding feelings which might be associated with your sounds and sights. You can develop a full visual, auditory and kinesthetic representation with practice.

II.   Development of Kinesthetic Ability

a.   Sit comfortably and go inside.

b.   Remember a pleasant experience and begin to feel it.

c.   As you are deepening the feelings associated with the experience notice the subtle changes in your physiology and continue to deepen your awareness of the experience.

d.   When you reach a certain point in your comfort, look for any snatches of color or movement that go with the feelings. Listen for any sounds that go with your feelings.

e.   Notice which feelings specifically cause you to have small flashes of pictures. Go to these feelings and stay there awhile. Develop any bit of a picture. If it is a color, intensify it. If it is a shape, sharpen it. If it is movement, slow it down till you can clearly see what is moving.

f.   Continue playing with these elements till you get more building blocks with which you can build a full picture.

The general pattern here is called synesthesia. This is jumping from one system which is caused by operation in another. Use your strength in one main system to develop a memory. Transfer to your next strongest system to further develop your representation of the experience. Finally, use the resources of your two stronger representational systems to bring in the elements of your weakest system. You can use this pattern to develop any weak system starting from any stronger system. I will leave the specifics of getting to kinesthetic representations from visual and auditory to your abilities to generalize the above examples.

SYNESTHESIA - OVERLAP

Please circle the letter of the response which matches the overlap of representational systems.

1.   Listening to her sends shivers down my spine.

    a.   Her looks give you goose bumps.

    b.   When she touches you, you melt.

    c.   Sounds as though it's a tingling experience.

2.   The warmth of this room rings true with our purpose.

    a.   The tone of this experience tells me we're on the right track.

    b.   It looks like we're really connected.

    c.   The feelings of this moment echo through these chambers.

3.   I'm hot on the scent of the solution.

    a.   Looks like you just have to nose around.

    b.   Don't cool off until you sniff it out.

    c.   I know you'll taste it if you get a whiff.

4.   My perspective gives me a firm grip on the situation.

    a.   What do you see that gives you such clarity?

    b.   Clarity often gives one a firm footing.

    c.   What is it that tells you that you're feeling clear?

5.   Your comments leave a bitter taste in my mouth.

    a.   Your words shrink in my mouth.

    b.   You sound sour to me.

    c.   That sounds fishy to me.

Each of the following sentences contain an overlap of representational systems. Generate your own sentence that matches the overlap.

1.   I want to share with you, but you appear too icy.

2.   That idea sounds like a brilliant solution.

3.   The harmony of this situation warms me up.

4.   Your gloomy appearance tunes me out.

5.   I feel all fired up when things look bright.

PARAMETERS OF INTERNAL PROCESSING

A.   Representational Systems

As mammals, human beings receive and represent information about their environment through specialized receptors and sense organs located throughout the nervous system. These preceptual modalities fall into five major categories:

1.   gustation (taste)

2.   olfaction (smell)

3.   vision (sight)

4.   audition (hearing)

5.   kinesthesis (body sensations,) which can be divided into:

   a.   somesthesis (tactile sensations)

   b.   proprioception or viscera (internal feelings).

In human beings the decision-making processes (the organization of behavior) is primarily mediated by the auditory, kinesthetic and visual representational systems.

Sensory representations can be generated externally by an individual's immediate sensory environment, or internally as with memory or imagination. In NLP it is important, although often difficult, to make an explicit distinction between an external setting or context and an individual's internal response to that context.

B.   Representational System Primacy

As an individual matures he/she learns to use or value the information provided by a particular representational system or combination of representational systems to cope with and make sense of different contexts in the sensory environment. Individuals, then, may be conditioned to use and rely upon a certain type of sensory information to organize their experience across contexts.

For example, a child will learn to pay attention to and make distinctions about different parts of his/her sensory experience if his/her parents hand him/her a pencil and paper and instruct the child to draw than if he/she is handed a football or a violin. If a large number of other factors in the child's internal (genetic) and external (social and ecological) environments direct the child's attention to information being received through a particular sensory modality, the child may be conditioned to rely on that information even in new situations where it would be more beneficial to pay attention to different sensory information.

C.   Lead Systems

A person may be very kinesthetic (i.e., make their decisions primarily from the way they feel about things) and yet receive information that they respond to visually. The visual images are transformed into feelings. This occurs through the process of synesthesia (the cross-modal or bi-modal representation of a particular experience).

In general, the **lead system** is the sensory modality through which information is brought to an organism's attention; the **primary representational system** is how that information is given meaning.

When humans generalize from learning to use a particular representational system during a specific task to using the representational system for an entire meaning-making reference system, this is known as **Learning II** or Learning to Learn.

D. **Identification of Lead System and Primary Representational System**

As a general rule "accessing cues" (that is, eye movements, breathing changes, interjections, and tonal changes) typically identify lead systems. Body types (size and tension), predicates and syntax, body position and overall tonality identify a person's primary representational system.

E. **Hemispheric Dominance and Lateralization**

In human beings the two hemispheres of the brain control the motor activity of opposite sides of the body. The left hemisphere controls the right side of the body, and the right hemisphere controls the left side of the body. Because individuals tend to specialize the coordination of many activities to one side of the body or the other (handedness, for example), one hemisphere may be dominant in the sense that its activity controls the dominant hand.

Although there is considerable overlap of sensations from the eyes and ears to the two hemispheres, the cognitive or perceptual systems (representational systems) governing the activity of the dominant hand tend to become lateralized as well. Most language functions, for example, are typically lateralized to the dominant hemisphere.

Typically, then, a person's primary representational system becomes lateralized to the dominant side while another representational system may mediate the other. For example, we have probably all heard someone say, "On the one hand this really looks like it would be fun, but on the other hand it just wouldn't feel right."

There is also evidence to support the idea that the hemispheres actually carry out different functions; the dominant hemisphere carrying out sequential cause-effect reasoning such as language and logic; the non-dominant responsible for the spatial, integrative, "artistic" behavior.

F. Limitations of Consciousness

It is obvious that an individual cannot pay attention to all his/her incoming sensory experience at once, although he/she may be able to respond to it automatically. Psychological tests have placed the limits to conscious attention at **7 +/- 2 chunks**. Much of a person's interaction with his/her environment occurs below the person's level of awareness.

Usually a person will be most aware of the information they are receiving through their lead system. It is very important in the process of NLP to be able to tell which of an individual's responses generally take place outside of that person's conscious awareness.

A state of consciousness is made up of the portions of a person's lead and representational system combinations in consciousness at a particular point in time. An altered state, then, would involve a change in a person's typical representational and lead system combinations.

G. Parts/Functions

Parts/functions evolve from the different behavioral responses an individual develops in different states of consciousness. As in the example: The same experience may look better than it would feel. It is possible to have as many different parts /functions as there are combinations of lead and representational systems.

For example, a child will learn to pay attention to and make distinctions about different parts of his/her sensory experience if his/her parents hand him/her a pencil and paper and instruct the child to draw than if he/she is handed a football or a violin. If a large number of other factors in the child's internal (genetic) and external (social and ecological) environments direct the child's attention to information being received through a particular sensory modality, the child may be conditioned to rely on that information even in new situations where it would be more beneficial to pay attention to different sensory information.

ACCESSING CUES - LEAD SYSTEM

1. **Eye Movement**: (see chart)

1.1 **Up and left** - access non-dominant hemisphere visualization (right-handed people); remembered or eidetic imagery.

1.2 **Up and right** - access dominant hemisphere visualization (right-handed people); constructed imagery.

1.3 **Level and to the left** - remembered sounds and "tape loops" (non-dominant hemisphere).

1.4 **Level and to the right** - auditory construction (dominant hemisphere); thinking of things to say, how to say it, etc.

1.5 **Down and left** - auditory digital; internal dialogue.

1.6 **Down and right** - accesses feelings; usually both tactile and visceral.

1.7 **Straight ahead** but defocused and/or dilated - quick access of any sensory information, although primary visual (generally the straight-ahead defocus will indicate which system the person has the most skill accessing).

2.   **Head Movements**: Head position corresponds to the eye positions listed above.

In general:

> **up** = visual
> **level** = auditory
> **down** = kinesthetic

Additionally:

> **left** = nondominant hemisphere
> **right** = dominant hemisphere.

3.   **Other Types of Eye Movements**:

3.1   **Squinting** - visualization.

3.2   **Blinking** - generally indicates visualization if blinking is somewhat prolonged, although it may indicate the access of other modalities depending on head position. Blinking will also often indicate the "punctuation" of information.

4.   **Breathing Changes**:

4.1   **Breathing high** in the chest or the cessation of breathing indicates visual accessing. Visualization is also characterized by shallow breathing.

4.2   **Deep breathing low** in the stomach area indicates kinesthetic accessing.

4.3   **Even breathing** in the diaphragm or with the whole chest and with a typically prolonged exhale indicates auditory accessing.

5.   <u>**Tonality Changes**</u>:

5.1 **High pitched, nasal** and/or strained tonality indicates access of visual information.

5.2 **Low, deep tonality** indicates kinesthetic access (except, of course, for certain emotionally charged memories). Voice is also more breathy.

5.3 **Clear, resonant** tonality indicates auditory access.

6.   <u>**Tempo Changes**</u>:

6.1 **Quick** burst of words and a generally fast tempo indicate visualization.

6.2 **Slow** tempo with long pauses indicates kinesthetic access.

6.3 **Even** rhythmic tempo indicates auditory access.

7.   <u>**Muscle Tonus Changes**</u>:

7.1 Muscle tension, particularly in the **shoulders and abdomen**, indicates visual accessing.

7.2 **Movement** indicates tactile kinesthetic accessing.

7.3 Muscle **relaxation** indicates internal visceral kinesthetic accessing.

7.4 **Even muscle tension** and minor rhythmic movements generally indicate auditory accessing.

8.   **Hand and Arm Positions**:

8.1   **Finger pointing** and/or **arm extended** indicate visual modality.

8.2   **Palm upturned** and arms bent and relaxed indicate kinesthetic access.

8.3   **Hands or arms folded** indicate auditory accessing.

8.4   **"Telephone" positions** (head tilted onto hand) and/or hands touching mouth or chin area indicate internal dialogue.

8.5   **"Counting fingers"** indicates access of dominant hemisphere, generally auditory digital.

9.   **Skin Color Changes**:

9.1   **Paling** or waning of color - visualization.

9.2   **Increased**, fuller color - kinesthetic access.

PHYSIOLOGICAL INDICATORS OF PRIMARY REPRESENTATIONAL SYSTEM

1. **Body Type:**

1.1   A **thin tense** body is characteristic of a visual person.

1.2   A **full soft** body is characteristic of a kinesthetic (internal) person. (People who are overweight are almost always kinesthetic.)

1.3   An **active muscular** body characterizes a person who is kinesthetic external; that is, tactilely sensitive.

1.4   An Auditory body tends to be **in between** that of a visual and a kinesthetic (the body will soften if the individual is aware of internal auditory information, more tense or tight if the focus of attention is external).

2.   **Predicates**: The predicates an individual uses to describe their experience will indicate the way in which they perceive and make sense of that experience.

2.1   **Visual:** I **see** what you are saying; That **looks** good; That idea isn't **clear**; I'm **hazy** about that; I went **blank**; Cast some **light** on the subject; Get a new **perspective**; an (**insightful, enlightening, colorful**) example.

2.2   **Kinesthetic**: If it **feels** right, do it; Get a **handle** on it; **Grasp** the concepts; Get in **touch** with yourself; A **solid** understanding; I'm up **against a wall**; Change your **standpoint**; You're **insensitive**; I have a **feeling** you're right.

2.3 **Auditory**: I **hear** you; That **rings a bell**; That **sounds** good; Everything just suddenly **clicked**; **Listen** to me; That idea's been **rattling** around in my head; Something **tells** me not to; I'm really getting **in tune** with that.

3. **Posture**:

3.1 **Visual**: shoulders hunched and neck extended (head separated from body). From a side view the body would be shaped somewhat like a question mark.

3.2 **Kinesthetic (internal)**: The head sits much more solidly on the shoulders which tend to droop. The body is well centered and to a certain extent blocky.

3.3 **Kinesthetic (external)**: Broad shoulders with straight athletic posture. The head solidly rests on the shoulders.

3.4 **Auditory**: Tendency for shoulders to slouch somewhat; head slightly tilted to one side; body tends to lean either slightly forward or slightly back (forward - external, back - internal). The person's arms are often folded or crossed.

4. **Virginia Satir's Communication Positions**:

4.1 **"Blaming"**: finger and arm extended, hunched shoulders, shrill tonality - visual.

4.2 **"Placating"**: dropping shoulders, palms upturned, soft or whiny tonality - kinesthetic internal (whiny tonality would indicate v/k split).

4.3 **"Super-Reasonable"**: arms folded, leaning back, robot-like tonality - auditory internal (digital).

4.4 **"Irrelevant"**: rapid cycling through all of the above characteristics - no stable representational system in stress.

5. **Occupation, Interests & Talents**: Individuals with a particular skill for or reliance on a certain modality will tend to sort themselves out in terms of what they do and what they are good at. Some examples are listed below:

5.1 **Visual**: Engineering and drafting, the visual arts (painting, drawing, etc.), Sciences (physics, mathematics, chemistry, etc.)

5.2 **Kinesthetic**: Athletics, tactile arts (sculpture, ceramics, etc.), manual labor (construction, nursing, housekeeping, cooking, etc.)

5.3 **Auditory**: Music, literary arts (writing, poetry, etc.), linguistics and languages.

Occupations and arts often are varied in terms of what sensory system they appeal to the most. Different schools of thought within a particular occupation may be indicative of different representational approaches. An art therapist or a therapist who concentrates on Jungian symbolism may tend to be more visual than a therapist who does Rolfing or Reichian body work. A psychoanalyst may be more auditory.

EYE ACCESSING CUES

While most people lump all of their internal information processing together and call it "thinking," Bandler and Grinder noted that it can be very useful to divide thinking into the different sensory modalities in which it occurs. When we process information internally, we can do it visually, auditorily, kinesthetically, olfactorily, or gustatorily. As you read the word "circus," you may know what it means by seeing images of circus rings, elephants, or trapeze artists; by hearing carnival music; by feeling excited; or by smelling and tasting popcorn or cotton candy. It is possible to access the meaning of a word in any one, or any combination, of the five sensory channels.

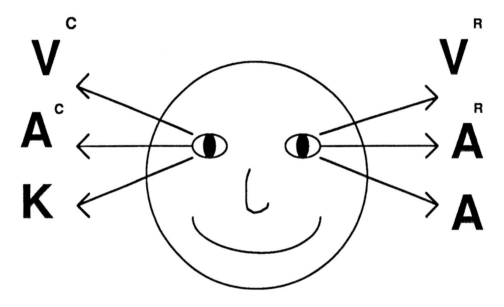

Trance formations. Grinder, J. and Bandler, R., edited by Connirae Andreas. © 1981 by Real People Press. Moab, Utah.

Bandler and Grinder observed that people move their eyes in systematic directions, depending upon the kind of thinking they are doing. These movements are called eye accessing cues. The illustration above indicates the kind of processing most people do when moving their eyes in a particular direction. A small percentage of individuals are "reversed," that is, they move their eyes in a mirror image of this chart. Eye accessing cues are discussed in Chapter I of Frogs into Princes, and an in-depth discussion of how this information can be used appears in Neuro-Linguistic Programming, Volume I.

This illustration is easiest to use if you simply superimpose it over someone's face, so that as you see him/her looking in a particular direction you can also visualize the label for that eye accessing cue.

Visual remembered: seeing images of things seen before, in the way they were seen before. Sample questions that usually elicit this kind of processing include: "What color are your mother's eyes?;" or "What does your coat look like?"

Visual constructed: seeing images of things never seen before, or seeing things differently than they were seen before. Questions that usually elicit this kind of processing include: "What would an orange hippopotamus with purple spots look like?;" or "What would you look like from the other side of the room?"

Auditory remembered: remembering sounds heard before. Questions that usually elicit this kind of processing include: "What's the last thing I said?;" or "What does your alarm clock sound like?"

Auditory constructed: hearing sounds not heard before. Questions that usually elicit this kind of processing include: "What would the sound of clapping turning into the sound of birds singing sound like?;" or "What would your name sound like backwards?"

Auditory digital: talking to oneself. Questions that usually elicit this kind of processing include: "Say something to yourself that you often say to yourself;" or "Recite the Pledge of Allegiance."

Kinesthetic: feeling emotions, tactile sensations (sense of touch), or proprioceptive feelings (feelings of muscle movement). Questions that usually elicit this kind of processing include: "What does it feel like to be happy?;" or "What is the feeling of touching a pine cone?;" or "What does it feel like to run?"

QUESTIONS FOR GATHERING INFORMATION ABOUT REPRESENTATIONAL SYSTEMS AND ACCESSING CUES:

Visual Remembered (Vr)

1. In your immediate family whose eyes are darkest?

2. Name four things that were on your desk the last time you saw it.

3. How many signs are on the front door of this school?

4. What kind of flowers did you last receive or give?

5. What color were the walls in your previous bedroom?

6. Who were the first five people you saw today?

Visual Constructed (Vc)

1. What color would you like your next car to be?

2. Can you see yourself with green hair?

3. Rearrange the furniture in your bedroom so that you can see all the furniture in a different place.

4. How much is 448 plus 26?

5. Imagine seeing yourself sitting here from a position 3 ft. behind yourself.

6. Describe how you would look in a clown's costume.

Auditory   (A)

1.   Can you remember the last excuse you had to make up?

2.   Listen to the first few notes of Beethoven's Fifth Symphony!

3.   Can you distinguish between the sound of a police siren and a fire engine siren?

4.   Whose voice do you have the most difficulty understanding on the telephone?

5.   When walking, which pair of shoes that you own makes the most noise?

6.   Sing to yourself the first few bars of the National Anthem!

Kinesthetic   (K)

1.   Can you remember the first time you fell in love?

2.   Which is warmer, your right or your left hand?

3.   Where is "reverse" in your car?

4.   When was the last time you overate?

5.   What is one of your happiest memories?

6.   Describe the "feeling" of your favorite article of clothing.

SUBMODALITIES

SUBMODALITY DISTINCTIONS

The list below is not complete, and the order of listing means nothing. Some of the distinctions listed are actually combinations of more basic distinctions: for instance, "sparkle" is made up of brightness, location, and duration. What distinctions do you make that you can add to this list?

Visual:

Brightness, size, magnification, color/black and white, saturation (vividness), hue or color balance, shape, location, distance, contrast, clarity, focus, duration, movement (slide/movie), speed, direction, 3-dimensional/flat, perspective or point of view, associated or dissociated, foreground/background (self/context), frequency or number (simultaneous and/or sequential; split screen or multiple images), frame/panorama (lens angle), aspect ratio (height to width), orientation (tilt, spin, etc.), density ("graininess" or "pixels"), transparent/opaque, strobe, direction of lighting, symmetry, horizontal or vertical hold, digital (words), sparkle, bulge . . .

Auditory:

Pitch, tempo (speed), volume, rhythm, continuous or interrupted, timbre or tonality, digital, associated or dissociated, duration, location, distance, contrast, figure/ground, clarity, number, symmetry, resonance with context, external/internal source, monaural/stereo . . .

Kinesthetic:

Pressure, location, extent, texture, temperature, movement, duration, intensity, shape, frequency (tempo), number . . .

One useful way to subdivide kinesthetic sensations is the following:

1. **Tactile**: the skin senses.

2. **Proprioceptive**: the muscle senses and other internal sensations of posture, breathing, etc.

3. **Evaluative meta-feelings** ABOUT other perceptions or representations, also called emotions, feelings, or visceral kinesthetics because they are usually represented in the abdomen and chest or along the mid-line of the torso. These feelings are not direct sensations/perceptions, but are representations <u>derived</u> from other sensations/perceptions.

Olfactory and Gustatory (smell and taste):

The terms used by psychophysics experimenters (sweet, sour, bitter, salt, burnt, aromatic, etc.) probably won't do you much good. The fading in or out (changes in intensity and/or duration) of a particular taste or smell that programmer indentified as relevant in the client's experience may be quite useful. Odors and tastes are very powerful anchors for states.

SUBMODALITY DISTINCTIONS AND CUES

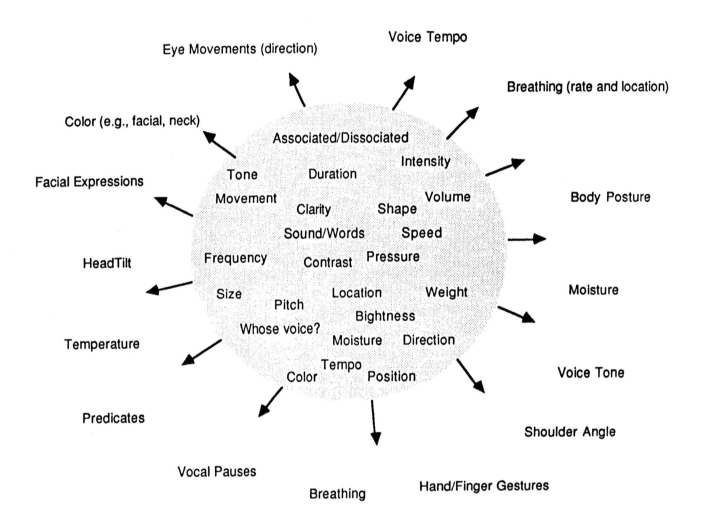

SUBMODALITY SHIFTS

Purpose: To show the effects on subjective experience of changing one or more submodality elements

I. Choose a pleasant experience, go inside and get a picture or movie of it. Discover the effects of changing each of the following:

2. Visual:

    a. Color: Vary the intensity of color from intense bright colors to black and white.

    b. Distance: Change from very close to far away.

    c. Depth: Vary the picture from a flat, two-dimensional photo to the full depth of three dimensions.

    d. Duration: Vary from a quick, fleeting appearance to a persistent image that stays for some time.

    e. Clarity: Change the picture from crystal-clear clarity of detail to fuzzy lack of distinction.

    f. Contrast: Adjust the difference between light and dark, from stark contrast to more continuous gradations of gray.

    g. Scope: Vary from a bounded picture within a frame to a panoramic picture that continues around behind your head, so that if you turn your head, you can see more of it.

    h. Movement: Change the picture from a still photo or slide to a movie.

    i. Speed: Adjust the speed of the movie from very slow to very fast.

    j. Hue: change the color balance. Increase the intensity of reds and decrease the blues and greens, for example.

k. Transparency: Make the image transparent, so that you can see what's beneath the surface.

l. Aspect ratio: Make a framed picture tall and narrow and then short and wide.

m. Orientation: Tilt the top of that picture away from you and then toward you.

n. Foreground/background: Vary the difference or separation between foreground (what interests you most) and background (the context that just happens to be there). Then try reversing it, so the background becomes interesting foreground.

o. Sparkle: Make individual objects in the scene sparkle.

p. Strobe: Make the whole picture strobe on and off. Make elements of the picture strobe.

q. Direction of lighting: Change the direction light comes from. Move the source and cause the shadows to change.

s. Associated or dissociated: Put yourself into the picture. Remove yourself from the picture.

t. Number of images: Split the single picture into multiple identical images. Arrange the images in a circle, a line off into infinity, or other shapes.

Experiment in the same way with each of the following:

3. Auditory:

Pitch	Distance	Tempo (Speed)
Volume	Rhythm	Continuous or interrupted
Timbre/Tonality	Digital (words)	Associated/Dissociated
Duration	Location	Contrast
Figure/Ground	Clarity	Number
Symmetry	Resonance w/Context	Monaural/Stereo
External/Internal Source		

SUBMODALITY DISTINCTIONS

The following sentences are interesting examples of the richness and uniqueness of human subjectivity collected from newspapers, magazines and conversations. For Neuro Linguistic Programmers, language provides a useful map for understanding another person's model of the world.

These sentences contain a variety of submodality distinctions and other sensory-specific words. Please do the following things with each sentence:

1. underline each sensory-specific word,

2. then indicate which representational system is presupposed by that word by putting a V, A, K, O, G above it,

3. indicate a word that refers to a submodality distinction by putting a SM under that word, and then

4. notate the sequence of representational systems presupposed by the statement.

                                    K   V   V
Example: __KV__ I can't get a handle on the clear meaning of hazy futuristic experiences.
                                  SM   SM

_____1.   I can see a need to tone down the loud babble in order to envision a brighter future.

_____2.   It's time to shrink the dark and overwhelming generalizations of the past that make it difficult to shed light on other choices.

_____3.   Heavy pressures can sometimes paint a glazed cacophony of sound.

_____4.   Black-and-white thinking can blind people to a colorful imagination.

_____5.   My relationship with him is so hot and heavy that I feel a need to distance myself.

_____6.   The harmony of warming changes speaks to me of sparkling horizons.

_____7.   Now you're ready to zoom in and narrow your focus to eliminate nagging obstructions.

_____8.   When your unconscious speaks to you, it's time to simulate a bird's-eye view of your life.

_____9.   You can now begin to clarify new circumstances to orchestrate work priorities for the coming months.

_____10.   It's helpful to drain your mind of cluttered images that leave a sour taste in your mouth.

STRATEGIES

STRATEGIES

All of our overt behavior is controlled by internal processing strategies. Each of us has a particular set of strategies for motivating ourself out of bed in the morning, for delegating job responsibilities to employees, for learning and teaching, for conducting business negotiations, and so on. Yet our cultural models do not explicitly teach us the specifics of the strategies that are required to achieve the behavioral goals expressed or implied by each model. Until the advent of NLP this was left almost exclusively to personal trial and error.

We may succeed magnificently with particular strategies (making money, for example), yet fail completely with others (personal relationships, for example). What, precisely, is it about strategies that generates successful outcomes in some instances and disastrous outcomes in other instances? By applying the techniques and procedures developed and described in NLP, individuals in many walks of life and professionals in many fields have learned to modify existing strategies or to create new ones for themselves and their associates to achieve exactly the outcomes they desire. The magic of success is a matter of employing the most effective strategies. Most strategies can be easily learned or modified to accomplish goals of our own choosing.

TOTEs and Strategies

The basic format we will use to describe a specific sequence of behavior is the TOTE (Test-Operate-Test-Exit), a model proposed by George Miller, Eugene Galanter and Karl Pribram in their book <u>Plans and the Structure of Behavior</u> (1960). <u>A TOTE is essentially a sequence of activities in our sensory representational systems that has become consolidated into a functional unit of behavior such that it is typically executed below the threshold of consciousness</u> (see <u>Patterns II</u>). As an example, a handshake for adults in western cultures is a single unit of behavior that often has the status of a TOTE.

The behavioral sequence that makes up a TOTE can range from the simple to the complex. For the beginning musician, the playing of a single note may be the largest chunk of behavior that he or she can handle. As the musician's skill increases, however, the performance of an entire scale or melody may be comfortably undertaken as a single unit of behavior - a complex sequence of activities that has become incorporated as a TOTE.

In our experience, the advantages of TOTE over other models for analyzing behavioral units are its elegance (it requires the fewest distinctions) and its incorporation of the important properties of *feedback* and *outcome*. Developed by Miller, Galanter and Pribram as an extension of the "reflex arc" (the stimulus-response concept) in behaviorist theory, the TOTE model retains the basic simplicity of its predecessor but far surpasses it in usefulness as a neurological model of the formal internal processing sequence triggered by a stimulus. That is, it extends the "reflex arc" model to include a feedback operation as an intermediate activity between the stimulus and the response. As Miller, Galanter and Pribram explain: "The **test** represents the conditions that have to be met *before* the response will occur." (p. 24)

If the conditions of the *test* phase (a comparision of the present state and desired state) are met, the action initiated by the stimulus *exits* to the next step in the chain of behavior. If not, there is a feedback phase in which the system **operates** to change some aspect of the stimulus or of the organism's internal state in an attempt to satisfy the test once again. The test-operate feedback loop may recycle many times before the test is passed and the action exists. (The TOTE will also exit if, after many trials, its operation phase fails to have any significant effect on the outcome of the test, although not to the same behavior as it would have if it had passed the test.) Miller, Galanter and Pribram write:

> . . . . .the response of the effector (the output neuron) depends on the outcome of the test and is most conveniently conceived of as an effort to modify the outcome of the test. The action is initiated by an "incongruity" between the state of the organism and the state that is being tested for, and the action persists until the incongruity is removed. The general pattern of the reflex action, therefore, is to test the input energies against some criteria established in the organism, to respond if the result of the test is to show an incongruity, and to continue to respond until the incongruity vanishes, at which time the reflex is terminated. Thus there is "feedback" from the result of the action to the testing phase, and we are confronted by a recursive loop. (pp. 25-26)

The TOTE process is represented visually by Miller, Galanter and Pribram as:

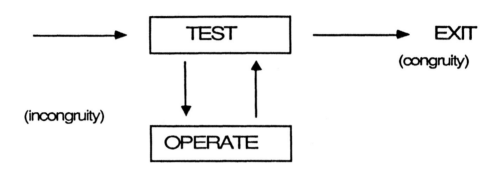

A simple example of a TOTE's test phase would be that of a threshold test. In this example the stimulus must be above or below a certain quantitative threshold value to satisfy the test for congruity before the TOTE will exit to the next step in the chain of behavior. If it is not, the organism will operate to increase or decrease either the stimulus or its own threshold level in order to pass the test. When you adjust the volume dial on your radio or stereo, you are performing a TOTE of this type. As you turn the knob, you continually test the sound volume by listening to it. If the volume is too low, you operate by turning the knob clockwise. If you overshoot and the volume becomes too loud, you operate by turning the knob counterclockwise to reduce the intensity of the sound. When you have adjusted the amplifier to the appropriate volume, you exit from the "volume-adjusting" TOTE and settle into your comfortable armchair to continue reading.

We can illustrate this example of the TOTE process in the following way:

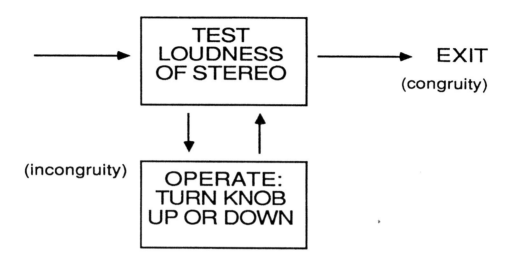

Applying resources to a present state of behavior in order to achieve a new outcome state (the three-step process we described earlier as the most general description of NLP), may also be represented as another example of the TOTE process:

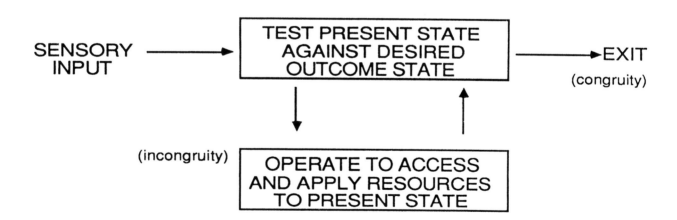

In this generalized illustration, the NLP practitioner repeatedly tests the present state of an individual, group or organization against a specific desired outcome state, continuing to access and apply resources to the system until the two states become congruent. The present state and the outcome state will be defined in terms of the distinctions available to the client (individual, group or organization) in each of the two states. The resources available to the client will be made up of the strategies in the client's repertoire and those in the programmer's repertoire, including the programmer's meta-strategies for modifying or replacing the client's strategies when necessary to achieve congruity in the two states. The operations involved in identifying, accessing and applying resource strategies will be presented in the following sections on Elicitation, Utilization, Design and Installation.

Elicitation

At a dinner party, the question, "How do you make such a delicious chicken cacciatore?" will elicit from the culinary artist of the house a precise sequence of steps - a specific strategy - for securing the outcome of a "delicious chicken cacciatore." If you miss part of the strategy (leave out a spice) or reverse two of its steps, it is most unlikely that you will later be able to achieve that particular gustatory outcome. Leaving out what generates the "m-m-m-mmm" response can result in an "ugh" response, a culinary disaster. On the other hand, once you've mastered the basic recipe, creative variations can produce delightfully rewarding outcomes.

Without question skill in the elicitation process provides access to a wealth of powerful and effective behavioral options that might otherwise remain as mysterious and elusive as the sensory specifics (V^i, A^i, K^i, O^i) behind the Mona Lisa's smile (judging from her accessing cues it's probably primarily A^i).

The Elicitation Process

By the word *elicitation* we mean the procedure the neurolinguistic programmer uses to gather the necessary information to make explicit the ordered sequence of representational system activity that constitutes a particular strategy. The first step in the process is, of course, to elicit, as a single behavioral unit, the strategy you would like to model, utilize and/or modify. There are two primary ways to elicit a strategy. First, and perhaps most commonly, it can be done **verbally**, through questioning. Secondly, a person may be asked to **carry out a task** which requires that he/she use the strategy in question. The second method has the advantages of less interference from introspection, memory and congruency check cues. To extract, unpack, break down and chunk the strategy into its individual steps two major tools of analysis are necessary:

1. A **vocabulary** - an explicit set of representational distinctions and a notational system with which to describe any particular sequence of human behavior (like that provided by the 4-tuple).

2. A set of sensory-grounded indicators or **behavioral signals** within the on-going behavior of any individual through which these representational distinctions may be identified. (These sensory-grounded indicators or behavioral signals are *potentially* available to the sensory experience of all members of the human species, but we have found that most individuals require a certain amount of training and practice before they become adept at it.)

Elicitating the Strategy

Many strategies will spontaneously and naturally appear during the course of a conversation or interaction; that is, _people do what they are talking about._ As a person talks to you about a problem, the outcome he/she desires, or any other aspect of experience, he/she will explicitly demonstrate, verbally and nonverbally, the strategies ordinarily used to access and make sense of that experience. By being attentive and observant (sensory awareness and calibration) the programmer can reduce much of his or her work and effort in the elicitation process. As people talk about past decisions, they re-run their strategy steps for making those decisions, like the "instant replays" frequently shown on television sports programs. When an individual talks to you about a stressful experience he/she will cycle through the sequence of representations that lead to the stressful response. A person talking about his/her difficulty in learning will demonstrate to you the very sequence of representations that is giving them the problem.

Typically, however, the particular strategy that you wish to modify or to utilize as a resource is not immediately available to the individual. In such cases the programmer will need to draw upon his/her own resources to elicit the individual's strategy. There are a number of effective ways of doing this.

1.   One way to elicit a strategy is to physically place the person in the situation in which the strategy naturally occurs - to work **"on location"** or "at the scene of the crime," so to speak. The context in which the strategy was developed contains many natural anchors or triggers for that strategy. This kind of elicitation would include options like putting the psychiatric patient back with his/her family, the pianist at his/her piano, the mechanic in his/her shop, the artist in his/her studio, and so on. You can also gather much useful information with this method about the context, the environment in which the strategy occurs: you will be seeing, hearing and feeling the strategy in action. In some cases, however, this procedure may be inconvenient, costly or impossible to carry out.

2. Presenting, imitating or reproducing a **portion of the context** in which the strategy takes place will help elicit strategy. You might choose to mimic the tonality and gestures of the employer, for example, your client is having difficulty communicating, or of the sister with whom the client enjoys communicating (depending on the purpose for which you are eliciting the strategy). In <u>Structure of Magic II</u> an example is given in which a young mother came for help with a severe and uncontrollable habit of child beating. One of the authors elicited her strategy for child beating by mimicking that portion of her child's behavior which triggered the strategy. Once made explicit, the strategy was modified, and the woman's problem was solved. Play acting and **role playing** are other effective means of eliciting strategies using this general approach.

3. By having an individual **exaggerate** some **small portion** of the strategy available to them, you will assist that person in accessing the rest of the strategy through the process of transderivational search. The transderivational search is discussed in detail in **Patterns** I and II. It is essentially the process of <u>going back across</u> representations from someone's personal history, <u>representations that contributed to the development of some pattern</u> in the person's ongoing behavior. It may usefully be thought of as an age regression to some experience or series of experiences in our personal history that we wish to recover and apply to our ongoing experience to help us modify, cope with or make sense of it. Using our 4-tuple description of experience, we can illustrate the process in the following way:

(A_n, V_n, K_1, O_n) On-going experience

.   .   .   .
.   .   .   .
.   .   .   .
.   .   .   .

(A_3, V_3, K_1, O_3) Age 15

(A_2, V_2, K_1, O_1) Age 8

(A_1, V_1, K_1, O_1) Age 3 Initial experience establishing pattern of behavior.

Here, each 4-tuple is a full representation of some related experience from the client's personal history. In each case something in the context has accessed the same kinesthetic component (K_1) that was originally experienced in the 4-tuple established when the client was three years old. This kinesthetic component serves as the thread which ties all of the experiences together. As the individual exaggerates the kinesthetic component, increasing its relative intensity value, he or she will begin to trigger or anchor up the other components of the 4-tuple representations from the past, increasing their signals in the ongoing situation. For example, a client who was bothered by constant feelings of intense jealousy was assisted through the author's (Dilts, R.) use of transderivational search to go back in time and recover full 4-tuple experiences in which he had had that same "jealous feeling." The search stopped when the client was able to describe an incident that happened when he was three years old, in which he recalled screaming and crying because he did not want his mother and father to leave him with a babysitter. With the initial triggering experience (K_1) elicited, his strategy for becoming "jealous" was modified and he experienced no further problems. Any of the representational systems can provide the thread that links a number of 4-tuples together.

The process of transderivational search is, of course, constantly operating in the on-going experience of all people. We continually apply representations from our personal history to help us make sense of and deal with our present time/space experience. It is one of the basic methods for learning and understanding common to all members of the human species.

4. Perhaps the most frequently used approach in eliciting a person's strategy for a particular behavior is to **ask** him or her **direct questions** about that behavior. The questions we ask will trigger representations and strategies from the individual's personal history.

For example, if you want to elicit a person's motivation strategy, ask, "Has there ever been a time when you were really motivated to do something?," or "When was the last time you were really motivated?" Similarly, if you wish to elicit someone's creative strategy, simply ask, "What is it like when you are exceptionally creative?," or "Have you ever been in a situation where you were very creative?" As people answer these questions they will access, through transderivational search, the steps of the strategy in question.

Thus, to access someone's strategy for the behavioral outcome "X," you would simply ask questions such as:

"Can you tell me about a time when you were able to X?"

"What is it like to X?

"How do you X?"

"Have you ever X?"

"When were you best able to X?"

"How would you know if you could X?"

"What do you need to do to X?"

"What happens as you X?"

"When was the last time you X?"

If you want to elicit a strategy to serve as a resource to help someone develop more choices about a particular behavioral difficulty, you may also want to ask questions like, "Has there ever been a time when you didn't X?" Then, find out what was different about their strategies and experience at that time as compared to the person's on-going experience. Referring to the three-point process we presented earlier will provide a strong format within which to structure a specific procedure for elicitation in each individual case.

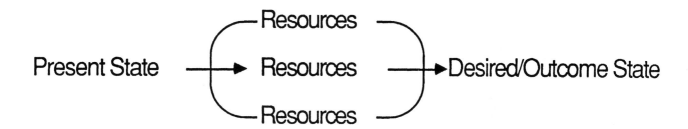

If, for example, someone tells you, "I just can't seem to do my work right, or get it in on time. . ." (present state), you can elicit a strategy to be used as a resource by asking, "Has there ever been a time when you were able to complete your work satisfactorily and comfortably by the appropriate deadline?" As the individual accesses and recounts this experience, he/she will also access and demonstrate a strategy useful in obtaining the outcome desired at this point in time.

Utilization

Utilization may usefully be described as the process of applying an existing strategy, one that you have elicited, for the purpose of assisting a client (individual, family, group or organization) in achieving some desired outcome, or in securing some outcome for yourself. Using this process, the NLP practitioner assists clients by running <u>new content through the formal</u> <u>representational sequence of an existing strategy by packaging or repackaging</u> the client's experience in terms of the existing structure of that strategy.

One of the major difficulties that people of all backgrounds and disciplines have in transforming the portions of experience with which they are confronted from the class of environmental variables to the class of decision variables, is that they have no explicit way of applying strategies and resources that they have used to successfully complete this transformation in past contexts to the on-going situations with which they are confronted. The process of utilization provides an explicit operation for making this transformation.

1. **Pacing Stratagies** - Pacing is the process of feeding back to a client, through your own behavior, the behaviors and strategies that you have observed in them - that is, by going to their model of the world. You will have successfully paced a person's strategy when you have packaged the information which you are working with (whether it is mathematical formulae, how to work camera equipment, making fiscal policy, etc.) such that the form of your presentation matches, step for step, the sequence of representations the person cycles through in that strategy. For example, consider the following strategy for decision making:

$$V \longrightarrow A_d^i \longrightarrow K^i \longrightarrow Exit$$

An example of a pace of this strategy during a presentation is: "I think you should take a good <u>look</u> at this, so you can <u>see</u> how it will fit into the whole <u>picture</u> (V). I'm sure you'll find that it will <u>answer</u> the <u>questions</u> we've all been asking (A_d^i) ourselves, and you'll really be able to <u>say</u>, 'Yes, this is the one!' You'll <u>feel</u> (K^i), as I did, that this is the most <u>solid</u> and <u>grounded</u> choice available."

Pacing is strengthened by using congruent hand leads, eye leads, posture leads, tonal leads, etc.

Identifying and Utlilizing Decision Points

The elicitation of a successful and appropriate outcome from a strategy will depend on your ability to help people satisfy specific tests that they have incorporated to organize and process aspects of their experience. Every strategy will have at least one step that functions as a <u>decision point</u> or <u>choice point</u>.

The decision point in the strategy is the step where the individual decides to:

    a)   exit from the strategy,

    b)   operate to change representational value in the strategy,

    c)   go on to the next step in the strategy, or

    d)   switch strategies if the one being employed is ineffective.

The purpose of all the information gathering and operations that we perform is to allow us to satisfy the tests or decision points in our strategies.

Consider the following diagram of the decision making strategy discussed earlier.

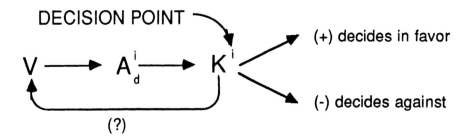

Here, the individual makes a decision by looking at possibilities, describing them to himself and then deriving internal feelings on the basis of those descriptions. The internal feelings constitute the decision point in the strategy. If the feelings are congruently positive (+), the person decides in favor of that particular verbal representation; if the feelings are congruently negative (-), the individual decides against it. If the feelings are ambivalent or incongruent (?), the individual operates by looking back at the options and by describing them again.

Depending, then, on the outcome you are working toward, you will want to emphasize different kinds of content representations at this step. If it is appropriate for the individual to decide in favor, you will emphasize a positive kinesthetic representation (+). If it would be useful for the individual to decide against, you will emphasize negative kinesthetic sensations (-). If you want many alernatives to be considered, then be sure to stress ambiguity in feelings (?).

Decision points, then, are steps in the strategy where different values of the representational system involved in that step (kinesthetic, visual, auditory or olfactory) will trigger different directions in the unfolding strategy sequence. What happens in the representational system at a decision point will have a great impact on the eventual outcome of the strategy.

2. **Anchoring - Accessing and Reaccessing Representations** - When it is important to control the content of a representational system, as when you are working with a decision point, you will need a way to assure easy access and reaccess to the particular representation associated with that decision point. This is accomplished through anchoring. Remember, an anchor is, in essence, any representation (internally or externally generated) which triggers another representation, 4-tuple or series of representations or 4-tuples (i.e., a strategy). A basic assumption behind anchoring is that all experiences are represented as gestalts of sensory information (4-tuples). Whenever any portion of a particular exerpience or 4-tuple is reintroduced, other portions of that experience will be reproduced to some degree. Any portion of a particular experience, then, may be used as an anchor to access another portion of that experience.

Establishing an anchor requires the setting up of a **synesthesia pattern**. "Synesthesia," as you recall, is the correlation between representations in two different sensory systems that have become associated in time and space. As we have pointed out before, a stimulus or representation is only "meaningful" in terms of the response it elicits in a particular individual.

Anchors may become established through any of our sensory modalities. Facial expressions (V), gestures (V), voice tonality and tempo (A_t), touches (K) and odors and tastes (O/G) can all be anchors for other representations. Internal sights, sounds, smells and feelings will also be anchors for other experiences. A strategy is a string of representations in which each representation is anchored to the one preceding it.

Design

Sometimes the organization or individual with whom the programmer is working will have no strategy immediately available for securing the desired outcome. Others may have strategies, which, although achieving the outcome, are very cumbersome and inefficient. Still others have developed strategies which achieved an outcome that was important and adaptive in one context in the organization's or individual's personal history, but which have been generalized to contexts in which the outcome is not appropriate. In this case, the strategy very often becomes **streamlined** and efficient but the outcome becomes maladaptive. Since the strategy is so streamlined that it is entirely unconscious, the individual or organization loses some of the requisite capability to discriminate in the test phase and, since everything happens so quickly, there is little room for flexibility. The person or organization becomes ineffectual.

In each of these instances the programmer may be called upon to help design a new strategy for the individual or organization in question. Some cases require a design for more appropriate tests; others need more effective and efficient operation designs. In cases where there is no existing strategy whatsoever, the programmer will have to design from scratch an entirely new sequence of representations.

1. **Streamlining** - Streamlining is required for strategies that are cumbersome or inefficient in achieving the desired outcome. For example, we have noticed that people who were good at reading aloud when they were children, or who are still good at sight reading, have a difficult time with speed reading. This is because they have developed a strategy that includes an auditory digital step in their processing of the written word; that is, they have a verbal translation phase in their reading strategy. Very fast readers do not have this step: the visual symbols making up the word directly access internal representations without the auditory digital step. The basic process is rehearsal.

2. **Redesigning Maladaptive Strategies and Outcomes** - In cases where strategies produce outcomes maladaptive for the contexts in which they occur, the programmer will modify the strategy or design a new one such that a more appropriate outcome is reached.

Phobias are interesting examples of such cases. A phobic response is an outcome of a strategy that was most likely adaptive for the individual at the establishment of the behavioral pattern. The negative kinesthetic response and withdrawal were probably important for the survival of the individual at some time because of other elements in the situation. And even though the quick phobic response will always insure survival, it becomes problematic in contexts where it is unnecessary or unwanted. More appropriate responses, such as uptime and alertness, are more efficient for ensuring adaptive outcomes.

Certain phobic responses are established when a very negative outcome, a result of the specific circumstances of an experience, becomes anchored to a certain situation or behavior that is then **generalized** to later situations or behaviors. Whenever the person is in a similar situation the negative experience is accessed, although there is no actual danger of a reoccurrence of the negative outcome. How is the fast phobia cure a design of a new strategy? In what system does it offer a new choice point?

3. **Designing Context Markers and Decision Points** - In some cases, where an older existing outcome and accompanying strategy have become inappropriate for a majority of circumstances, they may still remain effective for some contexts (even though these contexts may be extremely rare). The programmer will then want to leave the individual with a *choice* of accessing the old strategy as well as the new one. In these cases the programmer will want to install a test or decision point in which some representation serves as a **context marker** to indicate in which situation which strategy is appropriate. If such a measure is not taken, interference may occur as a result of ambiguities or overlap between the two contexts, which will tend to access both strategies at the same time. The person may not know which strategy to apply and may become immobilized by responding to both strategies simultaneously. Something *tells* him to do one thing but another *looks* or *feels* as if it would be more appropriate.

As a simple example of this, let's say you are working with a manager who has a strategy, when she sees one of her personnel making a mistake, of telling him (A^e) that that isn't the way the job should be done, after which she shows him how to do it properly (V^e). You design a new strategy which involves her pacing the employee posturally first, then explaining to the employee how she feels about the way the job should be done (K^i - A^c_d), and finally walking him through what she feels to be the appropriate behavior for the task (K^e). The old strategy is still appropriate, of course, for empoyees whose strategies are more visually oriented. The new strategy will be more effective with kinesthetically oriented personnel. The decision point, then, should involve a test that allows the manager to discriminate between individuals to determine which strategy would be more effective. A quick decision such as this can be readily based on a momentary observation of the body type, voice tonality, predicates and available accessing cues of the employee (V^e/A^c). The strategy that the manager chooses, then, is based on her observations of the employee.

4. **Artificial Design** - The purpose of artificial design is to create a strategy that will secure the designated outcome or outcomes in the most efficient and effective manner <u>when there is no appropriate strategy immediately available</u>. This requires that the strategy contain all of the necessary tests and operations needed to sequence the behavior and gather the information and feedback involved in obtaining the desired outcome.

One useful method of designing effective strategies is to find a person, group or organization (depending on which you are dealing with) that already has the ability to achieve the outcome you desire to attain, and to <u>use their strategy as a model</u> for your design task. If you want to be able to do well in physics, find someone who already has that ability and use their strategy as a model from which to design your own. If you want to be able to get outcomes in the fields of therapy, management or law, find the people who are already able to do this and use their strategies as a model. This way you will be assured that the strategy you are designing will be effective.

When designing strategies through modeling, one should be careful not to get stuck or stagnated with one particular model for doing things. Challenging the old limitations and models and creating new ones is the basic means for improvement available to us as a species. The NLP model itself is continually changing, transforming, and improving itself.

Well-Formedness Conditions for Artificial Design

As we have stated, the goal of artificial design in strategy work is to create the strategies that will most efficiently and effectively secure a particular outcome, which requires that the programmer discover:

1. what kind of **information** (for both input and feedback purposes) needs to be gathered, and in which representational systems, in order to achieve the outcome;

2. what kind of **tests**, distinctions, generalizations and associations need to be made in the processing of that information;

3. what specific **operations** and outputs need to be elicited by the individual or organization in order to achieve the outcome and

4. what is the most efficient and effective **sequence** in which all of these tests and operations should take place.

When you are tailoring your design to a specific client, it will be necessary to find out which abilities and resources are already present within the client's repertoire of behavior, which are missing, and which are needed. We have developed a set of **four general well-formedness conditions** for design to help you find what is present, missing or needed in your client's existing strategies, and which, if the conditions are met, will insure that the strategies you design will be efficient and effective:

1. **THE STRATEGY MUST HAVE AN EXPLICIT REPRESENTATION OF THE DESIGNATED OUTCOME.** If the strategy does not identify and get the specified outcome then it is useless.

   The test phase of the TOTE requires that the organism compare a representation of where they are now with where they desire to be. For this an explicit representation of the outcome is essential. How often when you've tried to help someone make a decision or implement some new behavior, have you asked questions like, "What do you want out of this interaction?;" or "How will you know if you've (changed, made a good decision, etc)?;" or "Where are you trying to go with all of this?;" and received answers like, "Well, I'd be happier;" "I'd just feel differently;" "Things would be better;" or "Things wouldn't be the way they are now." None of these responses provide enough information from which to build an adequate strategy. It is no wonder that such persons have been unable to achieve their "goals". Choosing the sensory systems with which to represent the desired outcome is a crucial step in the design of any strategy.

2. **ALL THREE MAJOR PRIMARY REPRESENTATIONAL SYSTEMS (V, A AND K) MUST BE INVOLVED IN THE STRATEGY SEQUENCE.** Each of our representational systems is capable of gathering and processing information that is not available to the others. We can perceive and organize things visually that we can not do kinesthetically or auditorily. We can sense and process things kinesthetically that we cannot do visually and auditorily and so on. This condition will insure that the resources of each system, and therefore of the organism, are at least potentially available.

3. **AFTER "N" MANY STEPS, MAKE SURE ONE OF THE MODIFIERS IS EXTERNAL.** This means that after so many steps in the strategy the individual should tune one of his/her representational systems to the <u>external environment.</u> This is to insure that the person or organization is getting feedback from their external context so they will be able to detect what effect the progress of the strategy is having and so they will not become caught up in their own internal experience. "N" will be determined by the kind of task being performed. If it is important to the carrying out of a task (such as basketball or therapy) that you gear your responses on the basis of actions taking place in your external environment, then put in an external check often. If the task requires more internal processing (like writing down an incident from memory or solving a complicated math problem) your external checks can take place less often. <u>If you are not certain how many external checks are required for a task, a good rule of thumb is,</u> **"When in doubt, put one in."**

4. **THERE SHOULD BE NO TWO-POINT LOOPS IN THE STRATEGY.** A two-point loop is a loop in the strategy where the individual cycles or spirals between two representational systems, the usual result being that the loop doesn't exit. The loop is kept from exiting due to an inadequate test or because the operate phase (which only involves one representation system) is too minimal to make any significant change in the value of the representation being tested for. Loops that do not exit can be established in strings of representations that display more than two points, of course, and these should be avoided as well. But the majority of spiraling cases occur in loops of only two points because they do not generally access enough information or behavior to form an effective TOTE. An example of a two-point loop would be when, during some strategy, an individual triggers an internal voice that criticizes him in a high pitched, blaming tonality. The blaming voice, in turn, triggers negative visceral feelings. The voice then blames the individual for feeling bad, and this causes the person to feel even worse. The voice then becomes further agitated and blaming, and the loop spirals between auditory and kinesthetic: A^i_d- $-K^i$. The same sort of interaction can happen among people in a family, group or organization as well. Notice that a change in any of the modifiers in a particular representational step qualifies as a new dimension. A change from auditory internal (A^i) to auditory external (A^e) would have kept this sequence from becoming a two-point loop. A change from tonal to digital, from remembered to constructed or from a polarity response to a meta reponse would each qualify as a legitimate difference in representational quality.

Rules of Thumb in Design

The purpose of design is to maximize efficiency and ease in achieving a particular outcome. There are other considerations that, although they are not well-formedness conditions, you should keep in mind while designing strategies:

1) When possible, *choose the strategy that has the* **fewest steps**: this is the **modeling elegance** rule: don't complicate the strategy if you don't need to.

2) *Having a* **choice** *is, in general , better than not having a choice -* this goes back to the law of requisite variety mentioned earlier; variability in behavior is essential to adaptation. This also refers to the point we made earlier that the old strategies you are redesigning may still be useful in some contexts. When working with NLP you should never have to "get rid" of anything, only contextualixe maladaptive behavior, and design and install effective strategies.

3) When possible, *opt for* **positivè motivation** *when designing strategies.* This is essentially an ecological consideration. Many individuals, and some institutions and organizations, have strategies that utilize negative motivation for achieving outcomes. Some people, for instance, have motivation or decision strategies that have tests that require a certain level of stress to be reached before the person will operate to access resources. The strategy keeps looping until enough stress is built up to anchor in a resource strategy. Others use punishment systems and aversive conditioning methods as motivators. And, although these methods are sometimes quite efficient and effective in securing outcomes in the short run, they will often end up being detrimental to the ecology of the person or system, because of the physiological effects of prolonged stress, pain, anger, and other negative visceral representations,. Also, we have found that negative anchors have a propensity to extinguish if not reinforced. Positive anchors, on the other hand, build in their own reinforcement.

Meta-Outcomes

The topics of negative motivations and requisite variety are only two of a number of important ecological considerations that occur in strategy design. One of the most important questions to ask yourself when designing a strategy or choosing an outcome is, "Will it violate personal or organizational ecology?" Make sure that the strategy you design does not go directly against any other strategies that the client has. Sometimes there will be important reasons why an individual or organization hasn't achieved some particular outcome or developed a particular strategy.

Any given specific outcome or task is framed within the context of a higher order outcome, an organizing principle or "meta-outcome" for the system (ie., the individual or organization). A meta-outcome is one that organizes the behavior of the system in terms of general goals like the **preservation** and **survival**, **growth** and **evolution**, **protection**, **betterment**, **adaptation**, etc., of the system. To be ecological, any other outcome or strategy must contribute to these basic outcomes.

Installation

As we approach the final section, we are approaching the end of what may be viewed as the second act in a three-act play. Some appropriate portion of your life experience prior to reading this is act one, in which the main characters are introduced, the plot is established, and the tempo and pitch of the action have risen to create exactly the right degree of anticipation for act two. "Live" theater, for over 2,500 years, has provided one of the most powerful and exciting forms of entertainment available to the human species. The sensory encounter with living people - surrounding us in the audience as well as on stage - allows us to experience a range and variety of synesthesia patterns that we've learned to appreciate and value in the context of that altered state of consciousness commonly called "vicarious" experience.

In the second act of our play - this book - the characters and their interactions are revealed to a depth and extent not available to us on the level of act one, generating new levels of meaning to the dialogue, gestures and facial expressions of the characters and setting the stage for the launching of the most powerful act in the drama . . .act three. Under the impact of the insights, dialogues and outcomes of act two, the action in the third act takes a quantum jump to a new dimension of experience, leading the protagonist to the denouement of your choice - a meta choice if you wish.

For weeks prior to the first public performance of a stage play, the actors and actresses of the cast rehearse their lines before the watchful eyes and ears of the director, who may insist on certain body movements, gestures, facial expressions, tones of voice, rate and volumes of dialogue delivery and so forth to generate maximum effect in the eventual presentation before a "paying" audience. The _function of a director_, in part, _is to recognize, elicit and utilize the talent resources of each member of the cast to maximize his or her performance_. A discriminating theater-goer decides to attend a play as much on the basis of who the director is as well as the cast and author.

During rehearsal members of the cast anchor their on-stage entrances, exits, movements and dialogue lines to particular cues - words or actions immediately preceeding their own "parts" - until each scene and act flow as smoothly as the ongoing life experience it represents and emphasizes. The purpose of all preliminary work is to embed, to disguise, to render magically invisible in the flow of the performance another and more fundamental set of cues: a sequence of culturally rooted visual and auditory stimuli that evoke appropriate combinations of audience 4-tuples. By controlling the sequence, tempo, timing, variation and magnitude of audience internal kinesthetics during a stage play, the actors play their audience much as a musician plays an instrument. If it is done well, both audience and cast thoroughly enjoy their shared experience.

Whether art imitates life or life imitates art, effective installation is like the preparatory work that is integral to a successful performance. The NLP practitioner, like the director of the play, insures that _all cues are appropriately anchored and that each member of the cast has rehearsed until his performance is exactly tuned to achieve the desired outcome_ - only in this case you will write the script for your own third act.

There are _two basic ways to install a strategy sequence_ that you have designed:

1. through **anchoring** and inserting the steps of the strategy; and

2. through having the client **rehearse** (a form of self anchoring) the strategy sequence.

Although these two methods will be treated separately as we initially present them, they are best utilized in conjunction with one another - firing off the anchors you have established as you "walk" the person through the strategy.

The **goal of installation** is to make the strategy you have designed function as naturally and automatically as the existing strategy it is replacing. Each step in the strategy must automatically trigger the next. There are two major well-formedness conditions for installation that you will be testing for to insure that you have done effective work:

1. The entire strategy sequence must be available to the client as an **intact unit** so that each step is automatically tied to the next.

2. The strategy sequence must be tied to the **appropriate context** so that it is wired (anchored) to some stimulus (context marker) within the context that will initiate the strategy when the stimulus is introduced. This is to insure that the strategy will initiate itself at the appropriate time.

To install a strategy effectively you will have to interrupt or break the existing strategy at the appropriate place so that the new one may be inserted. Generally this is just a matter of timing, so that you begin the new strategy at the place in the existing sequence where the old strategy would have gone into operation. Sometimes, however, you will have to purposefully interrupt the existing strategy (if the synesthesia patterns are too ingrained or the strategy operates too quickly) before the new one can be effectively installed.

As you install the strategy you will also want to test its **ecological fit.** If you try to install a strategy that is somehow inappropriate or maladaptive for the client you will encounter interference phenomena such as **resistence** to the strategy or "sabotage" of the installation process. This test can be done by finding the *outcome sequitur* that which follows the outcome - what happens after the outcome has been achieved.

For instance, rather than simply designing and installing a strategy for a student to achieve the outcome of writing a term paper, we might also include a representation of what his experience would be like *after* the paper is finished as part of the outcome. Similarly, instead of having an alcoholic concentrate on the outcome of stopping his drinking habit, we would have him consider what he would be doing if he weren't drinking as part of his outcome. This type of maneuver can often automatically positively reframe the person's experience of the specific task he is trying to accomplish by putting it into perspective within a larger train of events. The ability or inability to achieve an outcome may be based on secondary gains or contextual conditions that are not uncovered until the outcome sequitur is explored.

STRATEGIES - AN OUTLINE

A. **Definition of Strategies** - The way that we sequence and order activity of the representation systems leads to different outcomes.

B. **Kinds of Strategies** - Decision, Learning, Motivation, Convincer, Creativity, Memory

C. **General Systems Mode**

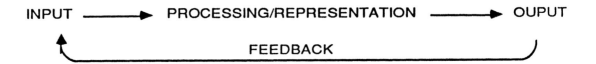

INPUT ⟶ PROCESSING/REPRESENTATION ⟶ OUPUT

FEEDBACK

D. **T.O.T.E. Model**

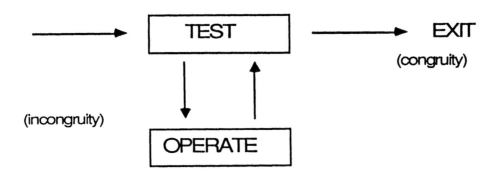

TEST ⟶ EXIT
(congruity)

(incongruity)

OPERATE

E.   **Revised T.O.T.E. Model**

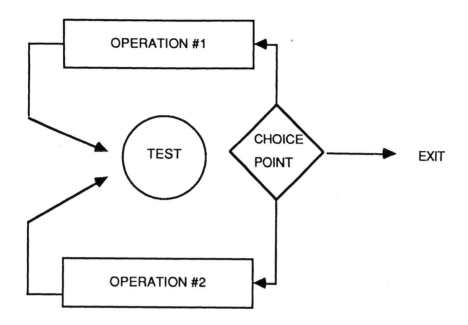

F.   **Fundamental Presuppostion of Strategies**: All behavior is the result of neurological patterns (i.e. sequences of representations within our representational system). If the neurological pattern occurs then the behavior occurs. If the neurological pattern does not occur then the behavior does not occur.

The particular neurological pattern is the result of two basic processes:

1.   Synesthesia Patterns - this includes things like anchors, associations, transderivational search and overlap; and

2.   Accessing Cues.

G.   **Strategy Elicitation**

1.   Use everything: predicates, accessing cues, breathing, tonality, etc.

2.   Put the person back into the situation. Don't remember, go back and <u>be there</u>.

3.   Basic questions: "How do you (know/think/etc.)?;" "And then?. . ."

4.   Make sure you get a logical sequence.

5.   If you're not sure of the sequence, try it several ways and find out which one generates the desired response.

6.   Notice loops.

7.   Make sure you get the key pieces of the strategy: the beginning and necessary middle pieces.

H.   **Structural Well-Formedness Conditions for Strategies**

1.   Strategy must have a well defined representation of the outcome.

2.   The strategy must involve all three of the major representational systems (Visual, Auditory, Kinesthetic).

3.   The strategy cannot cycle back before the Decision Point.

   a)   No loops without an exit point.

   b)   No two-point loops.

4.   Should have an external check after "N" many steps the strategy.

5.   Use least number of steps to get the desired outcome.

6.   A logical sequence.

I. **Functional Well-Formedness Conditions for Strategies**

1.   The strategy should have a **Test** - - A comparison of the Present State to the Desired State based on prestored or ad hoc criteria.

2.   The strategy should have a **Decision Point** - - A representation resulting from the congruence/incongruence of the Test comparison, the value of which determines the next step.

3.   The strategy should have an **Operation** - - A set chain of representational and motor activity for the purpose of altering the Present State in order to bring it closer to the Desired State. NOTE: Refer to the T.O.T.E. model on page 26 of this section.

The following flow chart represents the progression of a functionally well-formed strategy:

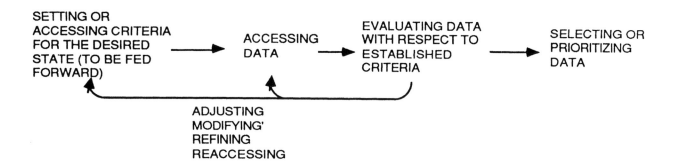

J.   **Installation Methods**

1.   Anchoring and Anchoring Formats

2.   Rehearsal

SYNTACTIC SYMBOLS

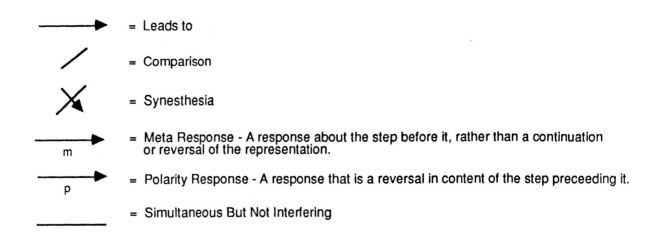

——————▶ = Leads to

⟋ = Comparison

✕ = Synesthesia

——m——▶ = Meta Response - A response about the step before it, rather than a continuation or reversal of the representation.

——p——▶ = Polarity Response - A response that is a reversal in content of the step preceeding it.

————— = Simultaneous But Not Interfering

Examples:

Sequence: $A^r \longrightarrow V^c \longrightarrow K^i$

Test: $V^e \diagup V^r$

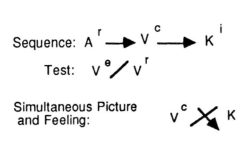

Simultaneous Picture and Feeling: $V^c \times K$

Saying one thing and Feeling another: $A^i \xrightarrow{p} K^i$

Talking about a Picture: $V^i \xrightarrow{m} A^i_d$

Inputting Auditory & Visual Simultaneously: $\dfrac{A^e}{V^e}$

STRATEGY QUESTIONS

GENERAL ELICITATION QUESTIONS:

1.   Think of a time when you were best able to learn something rapidly.

2.   Imagine some likely future situation and what you would do if you had to learn something quickly.

3.   What happens as you are learning something?

ELICITATION OF THE DECISION POINT:

For the response to a satisfactory test:

1.   How do you know when you've been able to successfully learn easily and effectively?

2.   When you're able to learn what lets you know you're done?

3.   Think of what it's like to be absolutely positive you've been able to learn something fully.

For an inconclusive test:

1.   What lets you know that you are not yet finished with your strategy to learn?

2.   What lets you know that you are ready to move on to something else?

3.   When you are not sure that you have successfully been able to learn something what lets you know?

ELICITATION OF THE TEST:

1.   What's a demonstration that you've successfully been able to learn quickly?

2.   What kind of comparison do you use to know you've succeeded?

3.   How do you test out whether you've achieved your desired outcome?

4.   How do you know whether you've done a good job or a bad job when you learn?

ELICITATION OF THE OPERATION:

1.   What do you do as you are preparing to learn something?

2.   What do you do when you're not sure you've met your criteria yet?

3.   What steps do you take to learn something quickly?

4.   What procedure do you go through to make sure you are ready to learn?

JOHN GRINDER'S SPEED READING STRATEGY

People using this technique can read non-technical materials at 4,000 to 6,000 words per minute with high accuracy and comprehension.

Existing Reading Strategy:

This strategy is appropriate for technical material.

$$V^e \longrightarrow A^i_d \longrightarrow ()$$ ( ) meaning 4-tuple

The existing reading strategy means that you can only read as fast as you can talk.

New Reading Strategy:

$$V^e \longrightarrow ()$$ ( ) meaning 4-tuple

Deleted A^i_d (audio digital step)

This strategy is not for reading large amounts of technical material, or for poetry!

How to do:

1. Pick appropriate non-technical material

2. Read the non-technical material the old way at the old speed. Test comprehension after waiting for a few minutes.

3. Negotiate with unconscious mind to displace the A^i_d component of the original strategy, noting that each strategy is appropriate for its own type of material. Accomplish in two steps: read for words, then consolidate for meaning.

4. Read 3 to 5 times the number of pages per minutes that you previously read without regard to comprehension in new style. Let eyes take in all words in large chunks, it may help to spiral your way down the page. Utilize new anchor (i.e. if you previously turned pages with your right hand then now turn them with your left. DO IT.

5. Consolidation for 20 minutes. Take a break! Leave the room, go out and think of other things.

6. Have another person ask you questions about what you read. They must use the eye accessing cues as confirmation that the material is in consciousness as a representational system. "Take a guess at material; belief systems may be present here". Start with large chunks using the meta model to specify "what specifically," forcing smaller and smaller chunks.

7. Use guide to start then calibrate for precision of what has been read. Level of understanding will be at least as good as the old way and probably better.

8. Practice for a couple days until it drops from conscious behavior.

People who use this method to read non-technical material and want to increase their speed build up a hunger for whatever they want to read. Building up to a demon state, handling the book but not opening it, they walk away until their desire is very great and then burst through the book, almost salivating in their desire to read it.

STRATEGIES - MODELING

Purpose: To elicit a strategy from someone you wish to model. To teach the ability to be a "behavioral thief."

1.   Someone has a behavior, "X," you want to model.

2.   Ask them to pretend he is going to X.

3.   As they go through the imagined experience of X-ing, you notice and record:

   a)   Physiology

   b)   Eye Accessing Cues

   c)   Breathing

   d)   Body Movements

   e)   Statements A is making about content

4.   Bring them back to the present.

5.   You now do what they just did: model predicates, physiology, breathing, etc. Fully install all of their behaviors. Any deficiencies in your target state can be noticed and corrected if you have an observer with you and/or if you don't get the desired outcome. If so, go through again. This time you might consider doing as your model is doing using micro-muscular movements.

6.   Test: As you fully develop the target state, does your model follow along? If your model does, you are probably very close to a full and true model of X. As you test, be sure your model is not recreating the state internally but is developing the state because of your interaction externally with him.

7.   Go forth and X.

LANGUAGE

THE STRUCTURE OF LANGUAGE

A number of people in the history of civilization have made this point: there is an irreducible difference between the world and our experience of it. We as human beings do not operate directly on the world. Each of us creates a representation of the world in which we live - that is, we create a **map** or **model** which we use to generate our behavior. Our representation of the world determines to a large degree what our experience of the world will be, how we will perceive the world, what choices we will see available to us as we live in the world.

> It must be remembered that the object of the world of ideas as a whole is not the portrayal of reality - this would be an utterly impossible task - but rather to provide us with an instrument for finding our way about more easily in the world.
> H. Vaihinger, The Philosophy of As If, (p.l5.)

No two human beings have exactly the same experiences. The model that we create to guide us in the world is based in part upon our experiences. Each of us may, then, create a different model of the world we share and thus come to live in a somewhat different reality.

> . . .important characteristics of maps should be noted. A map is not the territory it represents, but, if correct, it has a similar structure to the territory, which accounts for its usefulness. . .
> A. Korzybski, Science & Sanity, 4th ed., l958, (pp. 58-60.)

We want to make two points here. First, there is a necessary difference between the world and any particular model or representation of the world. Second, the models of the world that each of us creates will themselves be different. There are a number of ways in which this can be demonstrated. For our purposes we have divided them into three areas: neurological constraints, social constraints, and individual constraints .

EXPERIENCE AND PERCEPTION AS AN ACTIVE PROCESS

Neurological Constraints

Consider the human receptor systems: sight, hearing, touch, taste, and smell. There are physical phenomena which lie outside the limits of these five accepted sensory channels. For example, sound waves either below 20 cycles per second or above 20,000 cycles per second cannot be detected by human beings. Yet these physical phenomena are structurally the same as the physical waves which fall between these limiting figures: the physical waves which we call sound. In the human visual system, we are able to detect wave forms only between 380 and 680 milli-microns. Wave forms above or below these figures are not detectable by the human eye. Again, we perceive only a portion of a continuous physical phenomenon as determined by our genetically given neuro logical limitations.

The human body is sensitive to touch - to contact on the surface of the skin. The sense of touch provides an excellent example of the profound influence our own neurological system can have on our experience. In a series of experiments (Boring, 1957, pp.110-111) over a century ago, Weber found that our ability to perceive being touched at two points on the surface of our skin varied dramatically depending upon where on the human body the two points were located. The smallest distance between two points which are experienced as two separate points on the little finger must be expanded thirty times before the two points can be distinguished when applied to the upper arm. Thus, a whole range of identical, real-world stimulus situations are perceived as two totally different experiences solely as a function of our nervous system. When touched on the little finger, we experience it as being touched in two places, and on the upper arm as being touched in one place. The physical world remains constant and our experience of it shifts dramatically as a function of our nervous system. Thus, one way in which our models of the world will necessarily differ from the world itself is that our nervous system systematically **distorts** and **deletes** whole portions of the real world. This has the effect of reducing the range of possible human experience as well as introducing differences between what is actually going on in the world and our experience of it. Our genetically determined nervous system, thus, constitutes the first set of filters which distinguish the world - the territory - from our representations of the world - the map.

Social Constraints

> . . .The suggestion is that the function of the brain and nervous system and sense organs is in the main eliminative and not productive. Each person is, at each moment, capable of remembering all that has ever happened to him and of perceiving everything that is happening everywhere in the universe. The function of the brain and the nervous system is to protect us from being overwhelmed and confused by this mass of largely useless and irrelevant knowledge, by shutting out most of what we should otherwise perceive or remember at any moment, and leaving only that very small and special selection which is likely to be practically useful. According to such theory, each one of us is potentially Mind at Large. . .To make biological survival possible, Mind at Large has to be funnelled through the reducing valve of the brain and nervous system . What comes out the other end is a measly trickle of the kind of consciousness which will help us to stay alive on the surface of this particular planet. To formulate and express the contents of this reduced awareness, man has invented and endlessly elaborated upon those symbol-systems and implicit philosophies which we call languages. Every individual is at once the beneficiary and the victim of the linguistic tradition into which he has been born - the beneficiary in as much as language gives access to the accumulated record of other people's experience, the victim insofar as it confirms in him the belief that reduced awareness is the only awareness, and as it bedevils his sense of reality, so that he is all too apt to take his concepts for data, his words for actual things.
>
> Aldous Huxley, The Doors of Perception, 1954, (pp.22-23)

A second way in which our experience of the world differs from the world itself is through the set of social constraints or **filters** (prescription glasses). We refer to these as social genetic factors. By social genetics, we refer to all the categories or filters to which we are subject as members of a social system: our language, our accepted ways of perceiving, and all the socially agreed upon fictions.

Perhaps the most commonly recognized social genetic filter is our language system. Within any particular language system, for example, part of the richness of our experience is associated with the number of distinctions made in some area of our sensation. In Maidu, an American Indian language of Northern California, only three words are available to describe the color spectrum. They divide the spectrum as follows (the English words given are the closest approximations):

lak	tit	tulak
(red)	(green-blue)	(yellow-orange-brown)

While human beings are capable of making 7,500,000 different color distinctions in the visible color spectrum (Boring, 1957), the people who are native speakers of Maidu habitually group their experience into three categories supplied by their language. These three Maidu color terms cover the same range of real-world sensation which the eight (specific) color terms of English do. Here the point is that a person who speaks Maudi is characteristically conscious of only three categories of color experience while the English speaker has more categories and, therefore, more habitual perceptual distinctions. This means that, while English speakers will describe their experience of two objects as different (say, a yellow book and an orange book), speakers of Maidu will typically describe their experience of the identical real-world situation as being the same (two tulak books).

Unlike our neuro logical genetic limitations, those introduced by the social genetic filters are easily overcome. This is most clearly demonstrated by the fact that we are able to speak more than one language - that is, we are able to use more than one set of social linguistic categories or filters to organize our experience, to serve as our representation of the world. For example, take the ordinary sentence: The book is blue. Blue is the name that we, as native speakers of English, have learned to use to describe our experience of a certain portion of the continuum of visible light. Misled by the structure of our language, we come to assume that blue is a property of the object that we refer to as book rather than being the name which we have given our sensation.

The categories of experience which we share with other members of the social situation in which we live - for example, the common language which we share - are a second way in which our models of the world differ from the world itself.

Notice that in the case of neurological constraints, in normal circumstances, the neuro logical filters are the same for all human beings. This is the common basis of the experience that we share as members of the species. The social genetic filters are the same for the members of the same social-linguistic community; but there are a large number of different social-linguistic communities. Thus, the second set of filters begins to distinguish us from each other as human beings. Our experiences begin to differ more radically, giving rise to more dramatically different representations of the world. The third set of constraints - the individual constraints - are the basis for the most far-reaching differences among us as humans.

Individual Constraints

A third way in which our experience of the world can differ from the world itself is through a set of filters we call individual constraints. By individual constraints we refer to all the <u>representations we create as human beings based upon our unique personal history</u>. Every human being has a set of experiences which constitute his/her own personal history and are as unique to him/her as are his/her fingerprints. Just as every person has a set of distinct fingerprints, so too does each person have novel experiences of growing up and living; and no two life histories will ever be identical. Again, though they may have similarities, at least some aspects are different and unique to each person. The models or maps that we create in the process of living are based upon our individual experiences, and, since some aspects of our experiences will be unique to us as individuals, some parts of our model of the world will be singular to each of us. These uncommon ways in which each of us represents the world constitute a set of interests, habits, likes, dislikes, and rules for behavior which are distinctly our own. These differences in our experiences guarantee that each of us has a model of the world which in some way will be different from any other person's model of the world.

For example, identical twins might grow up together in the same home with the same parents, having almost identical experiences, but each, in the process of watching their parents relate to each other and to the rest of the family, might model their experiences differently. One might say, "My parents never loved each other very much. They always argued, and my twin sister was the favorite;" while the other might say, "My parents really cared about each other. They discussed everything extensively and they really favored my twin sister." Thus, even in the limiting case of identical twins, their experiences as persons will give rise to differences in the way they create their own models or perceptions of the world. In cases of unrelated persons, the differences created in personal models will be greater and more pervasive.

This third set of filters, the individual constraints, constitutes the basis for the profound differences among us and the way we create models of the world. These differences in our models can either be ones that alter our perceptions (socially given) in ways that enrich our experience and offer us more choices, or ones that impoverish our experience in ways that limit our ability to act effectively.

MODELS AND CHANGE

Almost every human being in our culture has a number of periods of **change** and **transition** which he/she must negotiate during the life cycle. Different forms of psychotherapy have developed various categories for these important transition/crisis points. What's peculiar is that some people are able to negotiate these periods of change with little difficulty, experiencing these periods as times of intense energy and creativity. Other people, faced with the same challenges, experience these periods as times of dread and pain - periods to be endured, when their primary concern is simple survival. The difference between these two groups appears to us to be primarily that the people who respond creatively to and cope effectively with this stress are people who have a rich representation or model of their situation, one in which they perceive a wide range of options in choosing their actions. The other people experience themselves as having few options, none of which are attractive to them - the "natural loser" game.

The question for us is: How is it possible for different human beings faced with the same world to have such different experiences? Our understanding is that this difference follows primarily from differences in the richness of their models. Thus the question becomes: How is it possible for human beings to maintain an impoverished model which causes them pain in the face of a multi-valued, rich, and complex world?

In coming to understand how it is that some people continue to cause themselves pain and anguish, it has been important for us to realize that they are not bad, crazy, or sick. They are, in fact, making the best choices from those of which they are aware, that is, the best choices available in their own particular model. In other words, human beings' behavior, no matter how bizarre it may first appear to be, makes sense when it is seen in the context of the choices generated by their model. The difficulty is not that they are making the wrong choice, but that they do not have enough choices - they don't have a richly focused image of the world. The most pervasive paradox of the human condition which we see is that the processes which allow us to survive, grow, change, and experience joy are the same processes which allow us to maintain an impoverished model of the world: our ability to manipulate symbols, that is, to create models. So the processes which allow us to accomplish the most extraordinary and unique human activities are the same processes which block our further growth if we commit the error of mistaking the model for the reality. We can identify three general mechanisms by which we do this: **Generalization, Deletion,** and **Distortion.**

Generalization is the process by which elements or pieces of a person's model become detached from their original experience and come to represent the entire category of which the experience is an example. Our ability to generalize is essential to coping with the world. For example, it is useful for us to be able to generalize from the experience of being burned when we touch a hot stove to a rule that hot stoves are not to be touched. But to generalize this experience to a perception that stoves are dangerous and, therefore, to refuse to be in the same room with one is to limit unnecessarily our movement in the world.

Suppose that the first few times a child is around a rocking chair, he leans on the back and falls over. He might create a rule for himself that rocking chairs are unstable and refuse to try them again. If this child's model of the world lumps rocking chairs with chairs in general, then all chairs fall under the rule: Don't lean on the back! Another child who creates a model which distinguishes rocking chairs from other kinds of chairs has more choices in her behavior. From her experience, she develops a new rule or generalization for using rocking chairs only - Don't lean on the back! - and, therefore, has a richer model and more choices.

The same process of generalization may lead a human being to establish a rule such as "Don't express feelings." In the context of a prisoner-of-war camp this rule may have a high survival value and will allow the person to avoid placing himself in a position of being punished. However, that person, using this same rule in a marriage, limits his potential for intimacy by excluding expressions which are useful in that relationship. This may lead him to have feelings of loneliness and disconnectedness. Here the person feels that he has no choice, since the possibility of expressing feelings is not available within his model.

The point is that the same rule will be useful or not, depending upon the context - that is, that there are no right generalizations, that each model must be evaluated in its context. Furthermore, this gives us a key to understanding human behavior - that key is, to see the person's behavior in the context in which it originated.

A second mechanism which we can use either to cope effectively or to defeat ourselves is **Deletion**. Deletion is a process by which we <u>selectively pay attention to certain dimensions</u> of our experience and <u>exclude others</u>. Take, for example, the ability that people have to filter out or exclude all other sound in a room full of people talking in order to listen to one particular person's voice. Using the same process, people are able to block themselves from hearing messages of caring from other people who are important to them. For example, a man who was convinced that he was not worth caring about complained to us (Grinder, J. and Bandler, R.) that his wife never gave him messages of caring. When we visited this man's home, we became aware that the man's wife did, indeed, express messages of caring to him. However, as these messages conflicted with the generalizations that the man had made about his own self-worth, he literally did not hear his wife. This was verified when we called the man's attention to some of these messages, and the man stated that he had not even heard his wife when she had said those things.

Deletion reduces the world to proportions which we feel capable of handling. The reduction may be useful in some contexts and yet be the source of pain for us in others.

The third modeling process is that of **Distortion**. Distortion is the process which allows us to <u>make shifts in our experience of sensory data</u>. Fantasy, for example, allows us to prepare for experiences which we may have before they occur. People will distort present reality when rehearsing a speech which they will later present. It is this process which has made possible all the artistic creations which we as humans have produced. A sky as represented in a painting by Van Gogh is possible only as Van Gogh was able to distort his perception of the time-place in which he was located at the moment of creation. Similarly, all the great novels, all the revolutionary discoveries of the sciences involve the ability to distort and misrepresent present reality. Using the same technique, people limit the richness of their experience. For example, when our friend mentioned earlier (who had made the generalization that he was not worth caring for) had the caring messages from his wife pointed out to him, he immediately distorted them. Specifically, each time that he heard a caring message that he had previously been deleting, he turned to us, smiling, and said, "She just says that because she wants something." In this way, the man was able to avoid allowing his experience to contradict the model of the world he had created, and he thereby prevented himself from having a richer representation, blocking himself from a more intimate and satisfying relationship with his wife.

A person who has at some time in his life been rejected makes the generalization that he's not worth caring for. As his model has this generalization, he either deletes caring messages or he reinterprets these messages as insincere. As he is unaware of any caring messages from others, he is able to maintain the generalization that he isn't worth caring about. This description is an example of the classic positive feedback loop: the self-fulfilling prophecy, or forward feedback (Pribram, 1967). <u>A person's generalizations or expectations filter out and distort his experience to make it consistent with those expectations</u>. As he has no experiences which challenge his generalizations, his expectations are confirmed and the cycle continues. In this way people maintain their impoverished models of the world.

SO WHAT?

The therapeutic "wizards" modeled by Bandler and Grinder came from various approaches to psychotherapy and used techniques that appeared to be dramatically different. They described the wonders they performed in terminologies so distinctive that their perceptions of what they did seemed to have nothing in common. Many times people have watched individuals working with someone and heard comments from onlookers which implied that these wizards of therapy make fantastic intuitive leaps which make their work incomprehensible. Yet, while the techniques of these wizards are different, they share one thing: <u>They introduce changes in their clients' models which allow their clients more options in their behavior</u>. What we see is that each of these wizards has a map or model for changing their clients' model of the world - i.e., a **Meta model** - which allows them to effectively expand and enrich their clients' models in some way that makes the clients' lives richer and more worth living.

The purpose of this section of your course of study in NLP is to present to you an explicit Meta model, that is, a Meta model which is learnable. We want to make this Meta model available to anyone who wishes to expand and enrich the skills they have as a communicator. Since one of the main ways in which we can come to know and understand others is through language, and since language is also one of the primary ways all humans model their experiences, we have focused our work on the language of change. Fortunately, an explicit model of the structure of language has been developed by transformational grammarians, independent of the context of psychology. Adapted for use in effective communication, it offers us an explicit Meta model for the enrichment and expansion of our communication skills and offers us a valuable set of tools to increase our effectiveness and our ability to bring about change in ourselves and others. The webs that you can tie and untie are at your command if only you pay attention to what you already have (language) and the structure of the incantations for growth which we will present.

QUIZ!

Which of the following is an example of a generalization, deletion, and distortion?

1. When she was in college Jamie paid careful attention to each problem marked wrong on her tests which resulted in hours of work redoing each of those problems. She graduated with high honors and got a job in which she soon was promoted to the position of Superintendent.

    During a meeting with her Department Manager he said, "Jamie, I think you're a hard worker; you've demonstrated tenacity, team work and creativity. The one area in which you could use improvement is in your performance appraisals."

    Jamie went home that evening depressed and told her husband that her boss thought she was doing a poor job. Her husband got upset and told her she'd be better off working where she was appreciated.

2. One day Sam, a Unit Manager, mentioned to one of his Superintendents, Steve, "We need more teamwork around here!" Steve, while having coffee with two other Superintendents asked if they had heard the recent complaint from their Unit Manager, i.e., that, "we don't know how to talk to each other - we don't have teamwork around here." At the next morning meeting, one of the Superintendents confronts Sam and says, "Because we're continually accused of not caring about our shift's overall operation and have to defend ourselves, our supervisors are complaining that they're not getting enough support."

3. Joe was a superintendent at his previous job for ten years. In his third year, during the early seventies, his plant was located in a city which had been the center of a great deal of controversy regarding racial prejudice. During a grievance proceeding, Joe was accused of being a racist. He did not believe that he had operated any differently during the proceedings than he usually did. Somehow the case was publicized in an insensitive manner in the local newspapers and the accusations against Joe were repeated. He kept his job but was transferred to a different plant by his company.

    Several years later Joe was promoted to Unit Manager. His Department Manager was approached by his superiors who were questioning why Joe had never been recommended for promotion by any supervisors who were Black.

THE META MODEL

All the accomplishments of the human race, both positive and negative, have involved the use of language. We as human beings use our language in two ways. We use it first of all to **represent our experience** - we call this activity reasoning, thinking, fantasizing, rehearsing. When we are using language as a representational system, we are creating a model of our experience. This model of the world which we create by our representational use of language is based upon our perceptions of the world. Our perceptions are also partially determined by our model or representation in the ways we discussed earlier. Notice that, since we use language as a representational system, our linguistic representations are subject to the three universals of human modeling: Generalization, Deletion, and Distortion.

Secondly, we use our language to **communicate our model** or representation of the world to each other. When we use our language to communicate, we call it talking, discussing, writing, lecturing, singing. When we are using our language for communication, we are presenting our model to others.

When humans communicate - when we talk, discuss, write - we usually are not conscious of the process of selecting words to represent our experience. We are almost never conscious of the way in which we order and structure the words we select. Language so fills our world that we move through it as a fish swims through water. Although we have little or no consciousness of the way in which we form our communication, our activity - the process of using language - is highly structured. For example, if you select any sentence in this book and reverse the order of the words in that sentence, or number the words 1, 2, 3, and move every odd word to the right over the even numbered word next to it, the sequence of words you are left with is nonsense. By destroying the structure of the sentence, it no longer makes sense; it no longer represents a model of any experience. Take this last sentence as a demonstration example.

Original version: By destroying the structure of the sentence, it no longer makes sense; it no longer represents a model of any experience.

After reversing the word order: Experience any of model a represents longer no it; sense makes longer not it, sentence the of structure the destroying by.

After moving every odd numbered word to the right over the even numbered words: Destroying by structure the the of it sentence, longer no sense; makes no it represents longer model a any of experience.

To say that our communication, our language, is a system is to say that it has structure, that there is some set of rules which identify which sequences of words will make sense, will represent a model of our experience. In other words, creating a representation or communicating is rule-governed behavior. Even though we are not normally aware of the structure in the process of representation and communication, that structure, the structure of language, can be understood in terms of regular patterns. The notion of human, rule-governed behavior is the key to understanding the way in which we use our language.

Language serves as a representational system for our experiences. Our possible experiences as humans are tremendously rich and complex. If language is adequately to fulfill its faction as a representational system, it must itself provide a rich and complex set of expressions to represent our possible experiences. Transformational grammarians have recognized that to approach the study of natural language systems by directly studying this rich and complex set of expressions would make their task overwhelming. They have chosen to study not the expressions themselves, but <u>the rules for forming these expressions (syntax).</u>

Transformational grammarians make the simplifying assumption that the rules for forming this set of rich expressions can be studied <u>independently of content</u>. For example, people who speak English as their native language make a consistent distinction between: (1) Colorless green ideas sleep furiously, and (2) Furiously sleep ideas green colorless. Even though there is something peculiar about the first group of words, people recognize that it is grammatical or well formed in some way that the second group of words is not. What we are demonstrating here is that people have consistent intuitions about the language they speak. By consistent intuitions, we mean that the same person presented with the same group of words today and a year from now will make the same judgments about whether they are a well-formed sentence of the language. Furthermore, different native speakers will make the same judgments about whether the same group of words is a sentence or not. These abilities are a classic example of human, rule-governed behavior. Although we are not conscious of how we are able to behave consistently, we nevertheless do so.

Transformational grammarians have created a model which represents that rule-governed behavior - those consistent intuitions about sentences. The formal model in linguistics provides a solution as to whether a particular group of words is a sentence, for example. The transformational model represents other kinds of linguistic intuitions also. Since the model is a description of human, rule-governed behavior, the way that we determine whether the rules of the model fit is by checking them against the intuitions available to every native speaker.

Native speakers have two kinds of consistent intuitions about every sentence of their language. They are able to determine how the smaller units, such as words, go together to make up the sentence (intuitions about the **constituent structure**) and also what a complete representation of the sentence would be (the **completeness of the logical representation**).

When humans wish to communicate their representation, their experience of the world, they form a complete linguistic representation of their experience; this is called the **Deep Structure** As they begin to speak, they make a series of choices (transformations) about the form in which they will communicate their experience. The choices are not, in general, conscious choices.

Our behavior in making these choices is, however, regular and rule-governed. The process of making this series of choices (a derivation) results in a **Surface Structure**- a sentence or sequence of words which we recognize as a well-formed group of words in our language. This Surface Structure itself can be viewed as a representation of the full linguistic representation the Deep Structure. The transformations change the structure of the Deep Structure, either deleting or changing the word order, but do not change the meaning.

The model of this process is a model of what we do when we represent and communicate our model - a model of a model - a **Meta model**. This Meta model represents our intuitions about our experience. The intuition of well-formedness is represented in the Meta model in that any sequence of words is well formed just in case there is a series of transformations (a derivation) which carries some Deep Structure into that sequence of words, a Surface Structure. Thus, the Meta model is an explicit representation of our unconscious, rule-governed behavior.

SUMMARY

Human language is a way of representing the world. Transformational Grammar is an explicit model of the process of representing and communicating that representation of the world. The mechanisms within Transformational Grammar are universal to all human beings and the way in which we represent our experience. The meaning which these processes represent is existential, infinitely rich and varied. The way in which these existential meanings are represented and communicated is rule-governed. Transformational Grammar models not the existential meaning, but the way that infinite set is formed - the rules of representations themselves.

The nervous system which is responsible for producing the representational system of language is the same nervous system by which humans produce every other model of the world - thinking, visual, kinesthetic, etc. The same principles of structure are operating in each of these systems. Thus the formal principles which linguists have identified as part of the representational system called language provide an explicit approach to understanding any system of human modeling. The Meta model developed by transformational grammarians was created to answer questions which are not immediately connected with the way that humans change; not all portions of it are equally useful. Thus, we have adapted the model, selecting only the portions relevant for our purposes and arranging them in a system appropriate for our objective of understanding what an individual is representing (the Deep Structure) in order to build a relationship and/or stimulate change in ourselves or others.

SENSORY-BASED DESCRIPTIONS - QUIZ

In the following list of observations, some are high quality sensory based descriptions, while others, without any other information, are not sensory-based and border on hallucination. Place a check mark next to each description that is a sensory-based description.

_____ 1.   The muscles on her face tightened.

_____ 2.   She was relieved.

_____ 3.   He appeared anxious.

_____ 4.   He became angered and lost control.

_____ 5.   Her face flushed.

_____ 6.   He looked down and to the right.

_____ 7.   She showed remorse.

_____ 8.   His pupils dilated.

_____ 9.   She acted uncooperatively.

_____ 10.   He acted in an immature fashion.

COMMUNICATION CHANNELS

Of the five senses only three constitute the major channels through which people communicate about their experience, either internally or externally. These three channels are:

VISUAL (see)

AUDITORY (hear)

KINESTHETIC (feel)

People either see images (or pictures) about their experience (Visual),

. . . Or . . .

They hear or talk about their experience (Auditory),

. . . Or . . .

They have feelings about their experience (Kinesthetic).

We refer to these communication channels as also being sensory channels. How people represent their experience (or model of the world) will be precisely the same way in which they will communicate about those experiences. Each person has a **primary**, or most prized, **communication channel**. They have a **secondary channel**, and the **third channel** is usually shut out of awareness. Generally, people will utilize their primary and secondary channels, except in times of stress; then, they will resort to their primary channel (or system), shutting out of consciousness (awareness) the other two channels entirely.

By conscious and unconscious, we are merely using a way of describing events that are useful in the context of communication. **Conscious** is defined as whatever you are aware of at any given moment of time. **Unconscious** is everything else. Finer distinctions are made, of course, and these will be discussed later in the training.

What's important is understanding the meaning of sensory experience. Sensory experience is the ability to quiet the internal channels, while keeping ALL of the external channels open and receptive to what's going on around you. The degree to which you are in sensory experience is the degree to which you will elicit the OUTCOMES (or responses) you want.

PREDICATES

Predicates are the process words (verbs, adjectives, adverbs) which people use to communicate about their experience (or model of the world). If you pay attention to this information, you can alter your own behavior (your choice of words) to "match" their predicates in order to get the OUTCOME (or response) that you want. <u>Generally what people want more than anything else is for you to understand their internal world</u>. What more effective way for you to do this than to communicate in the language of their internal world! If you want immediate rapport and trust with someone, one of the things you will do is to "match" them, speaking in the same predicates in which they are speaking. Conversely, if you want to alienate them (or break rapport), you will deliberately "mis-match" their predicates.

Predicates (verbs, adjectives, adverbs) are divided into the same three categories as are the major communication channels:

VISUAL (see)	**AUDITORY** (hear)	**KINESTHETIC** (feel)
perspective	listen	touch
picture	say	grasp
look	talk	handle
focus	voice	firm
clear	sound	concrete

If a person represents his experience (or model of the world) visually, then he will speak in visual predicates. Many of us speak in the same predicates as others, thus we find ourselves "matching" one another, deeply absorbed in conversation, and yet, there are those times when we "mismatch" the other person's predicates and then we wonder what it was we said that "offended" or "lost" the other person. Herein lies the difference between those people who are able to establish rapport and trust and those who are not.

PREDICATES TRANSLATED ACROSS SYSTEMS

UNSPECIFIED	V	A	K
attitude	perspective/viewpoint	comment/opinion	stance
consider	illuminate	sound out	feel out
persevere	see through	hear out	carry through/ stick with
demonstrate	show	explain	sort out
emit	radiate/sparkle	resonate	vibrate
absent	blank	dumbfounded/silence	numb
plain	lackluster	flat/muted	dull
ostentatious	flashy/colorful/showy	loud/smashing	slick/striking
attentive	look after/keep an eye on	listen in on	care for
ignore	overlook	tune out	pass over/let slide/ be insensitive
display	show off	sound off	put on parade
notice	look around	listen in	lead through
go over	look over	talk over	walk through
identify	point out	call attention to	put finger on
lay out	illustrate	talk (someone) through	move (someone) through direct
conceive	imagine	call up (recall)	get a hold of
remind one of	look familiar	ring a bell	strikes one
repeat	review	rehearse	rerun
refer to	point to	allude to	touch upon
insensitive	blind	deaf	unfeeling

SELF-PACED LISTENING EXERCISE

Say aloud (or have someone say aloud to you) each phrase below. Mark each of the phrases as being an example of either the visual (V), kinesthetic (K), auditory (A), olfactory/gustatory (O), or unspecified (US) representational system, that is, unspecified with respect to one of the five senses. Please mark to the left of the phrase.

1. _____ stumbled on it

2. _____ that stinks

3. _____ raucous crowd

4. _____ hazy outlook

5. _____ enlightened thinking

6. _____ a true belief

7. _____ soured on it

8. _____ get a handle on it

9. _____ loudmouth

10. _____ feel changed

11. _____ sticky situation

12. _____ completely in the dark

13. _____ shrill voice

14. _____ specific results

15. _____ unstated meaning

16. _____ colorful ideas

17. _____ quiet man

18. _____ think smart

19. _____ bitter notion

20. _____ harmonious relationship

21. _____ different horizons

22. _____ was pressured

23. _____ warming trend

24. _____ keep in tune

25. _____ yummy solution

26. _____ get the picture

27. _____ the best ever

28. _____ hidden costs

29. _____ hot on the trail

30. _____ lasting scent

ANSWERS: 1 (K), 2 (O), 3 (A), 4 (V), 5 (V), 6 (US), 7 (O), 8 (K), 9 (A), 10 (K), 11 (K), 12 (V), 13 (A), 14 (US), 15 (A), 16 (V), 17 (A), 18 (US), 19 (O), 20 (A), 21 (V), 22 (K), 23 (K), 24 (A), 25 (O), 26 (V), 27 (US), 28 (V), 29 (K), 30 (O)

MATCHING PREDICATES

	VISUAL	AUDITORY	KINESTHETIC
I understand you.	I see what you are saying.	I hear you too clearly.	What you are saying feels right to me.
I know.	I see what you mean.	That clicks.	I can grasp what you are saying.
	That's clear to me.	I'm in tune with what you are saying.	That fits.
	I have gained insight	That rings a bell.	I catch the idea, catch your drift.
	That's perfectly lucid.		That strikes me as being correct.
That's confusing.	Show it to me in black and white.	I can't make rhyme or reason out of it.	I'm trying to take it all in.
I don't understand.	It's obscure dim cloudy dark unclear inscrutable hazy clear as mud.	It sounds distorted.	It doesn't fit.
		It sounds garbled.	I'm straining to understand.
		It doesn't click.	
		That's a lot of gibberish.	It's impenetrable.
		It's Greek to me.	I'm groping for an idea.
			It has slipped away from me.

"MATCHING THE OTHER PARTY"

The following are statements from subordinates. On the answer sheet, indicate with the letter of the response you, as the boss, might make to match the representational systems used by the subordinate.

1. Everything is unclear. I want to see what's in store for us.

   a. Let's clear away the fog so you can come to grips with your situation.
   b. Sounds like you just can't hear yourself think.
   c. I want to show you how to shine some light on your future.
   d. Yes, and what's more important are the feelings behind that lack of clarity.

2. I can't grasp what you're saying.

   a. Let me say it more clearly.
   b. Let me say it another way so you can get a handle on it.
   c. Could you grasp it if I sketched it a bit more clearly for you?
   d. What specifically can't you see?

3. Things just don't seem to click.

   a. What specifically are you having trouble tuning in to?
   b. I can see what you're saying.
   c. How specifically aren't they working?
   d. What things specifically can't you see clearly?

4. I can't seem to focus on my sense of the problem.

   a. What stops you from getting a handle on it?
   b. What feelings specifically can't you tune in to?
   c. How would it look to you if you had a handle on it?
   d. What would happen if you could tune in to it?

5.   I get too much static from the VP.

  a.   Noisy turkey, isn't she?
  b.   She's always jumping on your case.
  c.   How does she make you feel uncomfortable?
  d.   You feel the VP doesn't like you at all.

6.   The warmth is gone from my marriage.

  a.   Clear this up for me: You'd like to relate better in what ways?
  b.   How would you like to rekindle the fire?
  c.   How, specifically, are you out of tune?
  d.   The two of you haven't seen eye-to-eye for a long time.

ANSWERS: 1 (c), 2 (b), 3 (a), 4 (c), 5 (a), 6 (b)

PREDICATES

Each of the following sentences contain one or more predicates that presuppose a specific sensory representation. First, identify the appropriate representational system by writing a sentence containing at least one predicate matching the form of the original sentence. Then, write two additional sentences that are translations of the original sentence into two different representational systems.

For example: That idea doesn't hold water.

                Match: That idea doesn't have a leg to stand on.
                Trans: That idea doesn't focus on essentials.
                Trans: That idea doesn't ring a bell.

1.   I can envision a brighter tomorrow.

    Match:

    Trans:

    Trans:

2.   She has a fresh taste for knowledge.

    Match:

    Trans:

    Trans:

3.   Your plan sounds like music to my ears.

    Match:

    Trans:

    Trans:

4.   Sometimes you need to sniff around for a good clue in cases like this.

     Match:

     Trans:

     Trans:

5.   If you can swing it, let's go tomorrow.

     Match:

     Trans:

     Trans:

6.   Diplomatic negotiations can orchestrate a harmonious peace.

     Match:

     Trans:

     Trans:

7.   Your proposal offers many colorful possibilities for increasing sales.

     Match:

     Trans:

     Trans:

THE META MODEL

The Meta Model was developed by John Grinder and Richard Bandler to identify classes of natural language patterns as a means to help increase the flow of information between human beings. Because we do not operate directly on the world we live in, we create models or maps of the world which we use to guide our behavior. As an effective communicator it is crucial to understand another's "map of the world" and the Meta Model provides techniques for gathering this information. These "maps" are not good or bad, right or wrong; they either empower us or limit us. Our goal is to be sure that language empowers us, and discovering what sensory experiences are associated with words can shed some light on how we limit this empowering and provide information which will allow us to change our models of the world.

The basic premise is that words (Surface Structure) are meaningful only in that they associate (anchor) in an individual some sensory representation (Deep Structure). During the codification of sensory experience into words (as an individual speaks) and the process of decoding (as a second individual listens and transforms the auditory stimulus into his/her own sensory representation) important information can be lost or distorted.

As previously stated in this manual, attention to non-verbal gestures and behavior and to context is critical during communication. The Meta Model provides you with language to attend to during an interaction which will bring higher quality information.

The Meta Model distinctions fall into three natural groupings:

Gathering Information

Limits of the Speaker's Model

Semantic Ill-formedness

META MODEL I - GATHERING INFORMATION

Gathering information refers to gaining, through appropriate questions and responses, an accurate and full reconnecting the speaker's language with his or her experience. There are four distinctions in this category:

Deletion

Lack of Referential Index

Unspecified Verbs

Nominalizations

DELETION

Simple deletion is when some object, person or event (noun phrases or noun argument) has been left out of the surface structure. The goal in recovering the deleted information is to gain a fuller representation of the experience of the speaker. To recover this information you ask: **ABOUT WHOM?** or **ABOUT WHAT?** For example:

"I'm really uncomfortable".
(response) "Uncomfortable about *what specifically?*"

"He's the best banker".
(response) "Between *whom?*"

In the case of deletion, asking the question, "How, specifically?" will give information concerning the representational system being used by the client.

"I don't understand".
(response) "*How, specifically* do you know you don't understand?"
"It's just not *clear* to me." (i.e. visual representation)

Step-by-step, the procedure can be outlined as follows:

Step 1:   Listen to the Surface Structure the client presents;

Step 2:   Identify the verbs in that Surface Structure;

Step 3:   Determine whether the verbs can occur in a sentence which is fuller - that is, has more arguments or noun phrases in it than the original.

LACK OF REFERENTIAL INDEX

Lack of referential index is when an object or person (noun) that is being referred to is unspecific. In this case of generalization the person has an experience out of perspective or out of proportion. To challenge a lack of referential index, ask: **WHO SPECIFICALLY?** or **WHAT SPECIFICALLY?** For example:

"She doesn't pay attention to what I say".
(response) "*Who specifically* is not attending?"

"That doesn't matter."
(response) "*What specifically* doesn't matter?"

Step-by-step, the procedure can be outlined as follows:

Step 1:   Listen to the client's Surface Structure, identifying each non-process word.

Step 2:   For each of these, ask yourself whether it picks out a specific person or thing in the world.

UNSPECIFIED VERBS

All verbs are relatively unspecified. However, "hold my hand" is more specific than "touch me." Unspecified verbs are verbs which are not entirely explicit where sometimes the action needs to be made more specific. Specifying the verb reconnects the speaker more fully to his/her experience. To challenge unspecified verbs, ask: **HOW SPECIFICALLY?** For example,

"She hurt me."
(response) "*How specifically* did she hurt you?"

"My supervisor hates me."
(response) "Hates you *how specifically*?"

Step-by-step, the procedure can be outlined as follows:

Step 1: Listen to the client's Surface Structure, identifying the process words or verbs.

Step 2: Ask yourself whether the image presented by the verb is "clear" enough for you to specify the actual sequence of events being described.

NOMINALIZATIONS

One of the ways people become immobilized is to turn an ongoing process into an event. Events are things which occur at one point in time and are finished. Once they occur, their outcomes are fixed and nothing can be done to change them. This way of representing experience is impoverishing in the sense that people lose control of ongoing processes by representing them as events. Identifying and challenging nominalizations is the linguistic mechanism for turning a process into an event. Bandler and Grinder say that specifically reversing nominalizations assists the person in coming to see that what s/he had considered an event finished and beyond his/her control is a continuing process which can be changed. There are two quick ways to distinguish nominalizations from regular nouns. You can visualize a **wheelbarrow,** and if the noun can not fit in the wheelbarrow it is a nominalization. For example, a cat, table, your sister can all fit in a wheelbarrow; however, love, frustration, communication can not fit in a wheelbarrow. Another way to **test for a nominalization** is to check whether the event word fits into the bland syntactic frame, "**an ongoing _____**":

an ongoing communication	nominalization
an ongoing table	
an ongoing frustration	nominalization
an ongoing sister	

To transform a nominalization back into a process word, **use it as a verb in the response:**

"Wake up!"
(response) "What do you want me to **wake-up** to?"

"I want help".
(response) "How do you want to be **helped**?"

Step-by-step, the procedure can be outlined as follows:

Step 1:   Listen to the Surface Structure presented by the client.

Step 2:   For each of the elements of the Surface Structure which is not a process word or verb, ask yourself whether it describes some event which is actually a process in the world, or ask yourself whether there is some verb which sounds/looks like it and is close to it in meaning.

Step 3:   Test to see whether the event word fits into the blank in the syntactic form, **an ongoing _____**.

META MODEL WORKSHEET I:

Directions: Circle the word or phrase in each sentence that represents the Meta model category; then write an appropriate challenge.

Referential Index   Words and phrases in the client's Surface Structure which do not have a referential index. If the word or phrase fails to pick out a specific person or thing, then the operator has identified a generalization.
Challenge: Who, specifically? or **What, specifically?**

1.   People push me around.

   _____

2.   Nobody pays attention to what I say.

   _____

3.   I always avoid situations I feel uncomfortable in.

   _____

4.   One should respect other's feelings.

   _____

5.   Everybody feels that way sometimes.

   _____

Nominalizations A process word or verb in the Deep Structure appears as an event word or noun in the Surface Structure. The purpose of recognizing nominalizations is to assist the client in reconnecting his linguistic model with the ongoing dynamic processes of life. So reversing nominalizations assists the client in coming to see that what he had considered as an event, finished beyond his control, is STILL an ongoing process that can be changed.
Challenge: Use the noun as a verb in the response:

1. My divorce is painful.

   _____

2. Our terror is blocking us.

   _____

3. My husband's laughter causes my anger.

   _____

4. Your refusal to leave here forces my departure.

   _____

5. Your perceptions are seriously wrong.

   _____

Unspecified Verbs   Verbs which lack the specificity needed to completely understand the full meaning intended in the communication.
Challenge: How, specifically?

1.   My mother hurt me.

   _____

2.   My children force me to punish them.

   _____

3.   Sharon is always demanding attention from me.

   _____

4.   I always show my spouse that I love him.

   _____

5.   My family is trying to drive me crazy.

   _____

THE META MODEL II - Limits of the Speaker's Model

UNIVERSAL QUANTIFIERS

Universal quantifiers refer to the set of words typified by **"all," "every," "always," "never," "nobody"**. They are words which generalize a few experiences to a whole class of experience. Emphasizing the generalization described by the speaker's universal quantifiers by exaggerating it - both by voice quality and by inserting additional universal quantifiers - serves to challenge them. Also, you can ask the speaker if they have had an experience that contradicts their own generalization.

"She never listens to me?"
(response) "How do you know that she *never* listens to you?"

"It is impossible to get anything done on time."
(response) "Has there *ever* been a time when you did get something done on time?"

Step-by-step, the procedure can be outlined as follows:

Step 1.   Listen to the client's Surface Structure, identifying universal quantifiers.

Step 2.   Challenge the universality of the generalization.

MODAL OPERATORS OF POSSIBILITY AND NECESSITY

Modal operators of possibility and necessity are statements identifying rules about or limits to an individual's behavior. Examples of possibility are **can/can't, possible/impossible, will/won't, may/may not**. Examples of necessity are **should/shouldn't, must, must not, have to**. To challenge these limits ask **WHAT STOPS YOU?** and/or **WHAT WOULD HAPPEN IF YOU DID?** The first response forces the person to think about what experience(s) they had that allowed this generalization to be formed. The later response requests the speaker think about consequences.

"I can't relax."
(response) *"What stops you?"*

"I shouldn't let them know how I feel about that."
(response) *"What would happen if you did?"*

Step-by-step, the procedure can be outlined as follows:

Step 1: Listen to the client; examine the client's Surface Structure for the presence of the cue words and phrases identified as modal operators.

Step 2: (a) If modal operators of necessity are present, use a question form asking for the deleted consequence or outcome of failing to do what the client's Surface Structure claims is necessary; or

(b) if the modal operators of possibility are present, use a question form asking for the deleted material which makes impossible what the client's Surface Structure claims is impossible.

LOST PERFORMATIVE

Lost Performatives are statements and **judgments** that an individual considers to be true about the world which may be generalizations based on the individual's own experience. They are characterized by words like: **good, bad, crazy, sick, right, wrong, true, false,** etc. To challenge a lost performative, ask: **FOR WHOM?**

"It's bad to be inconsistent."
(response) ***"Bad for whom?"***

"This is the right way to do it."
(response) **"This is the right way for whom to do it?"**

Step-by-step, the procedure can be outlined as follows:

Step 1: Listen to the client's Surface Structure for generalizations about the world - these are identified with the words "crazy, bad, good, correct, right, wrong, only, true, false."

Step 2: Identify that this is a generalization about the client's model of the world.

Step 3: Since this is a generalization about the model and not about the world, the effective communicator may help the client develop other options within his/her model.

META MODEL WORKSHEET II

Directions: Circle the word or phrase in the sentence that represents the Meta model category; then write an appropriate challenge.

Universal Quantifiers: Indicators of the extent to which certain generalizations apply.
Challenge: "Mark out" with tone, pitch, volume, and/or intensity the universal quantifier and **make it a question**.

1. You talk all the time!

   _____

2. Each day is the same old shit!

   _____

3. You never appreciate what I do!

   _____

4. None of the people liked me!

   _____

5. Nothing matters any more!

   _____

Modal Operators: These words express limits on the nouns and verbs in the sentence and constitute limits on the model itself. **Challenge: "What prevents you?;" or "What would happen if you did?"**

1.   People have to learn to be competent.

   _____

2.   I am unable to do these exercises.

   _____

3.   I must finish this project on time.

   _____

4.   Nobody is able to understand me.

   _____

5.   One should always take necessary precautions.

   _____

Lost Performatives: Statements in the form of generalizations about the world itself, which include judgments which are true of their model of the world.
Challenge: "For whom?;" "Who says?;" o r "How do you know?"

1. It's bad to be inconsistent.

   _____

2. Mature men don't cry.

   _____

3. It's crazy to not make a choice.

   _____

4. There is only one way to do this job right.

   _____

5. We can only increase sales by servicing our clients.

   _____

THE META MODEL III - SEMANTIC ILL-FORMEDNESS

CAUSE AND EFFECT

Cause-Effect is when an individual makes a causal linkage between their experience or response to some outside stimulus that is not necessarily directly connected, or where the connection is not clear. The challenge is one of asking, **"HOW DOES X CAUSE Y?"**

"This lecture makes me bored."
(response) **"How specifically does it *make* you bored?"**

"You irritate me."
(response) **"How do** I irritate you?" "How is it possible for me to irritate you?"
(or,". . . make you feel irritated?")

MIND READING

Mind-Reading is when an individual claims to know what another individual is thinking without having received any specific communication from the second individual. The challenge for this pattern is **"HOW SPECIFICALLY DO YOU KNOW X?"** This provides a way for the speaker to become aware of and even to question those assumptions she/he may have previously taken for granted.

"Henry never considers my feelings."
(response) **"How do you know** that Henry never considers your feelings?"

"I'm sure you can see how I feel?"
(response) **"How, specifically, can you be sure** I see how you feel?"

Step-by-step for challenging <u>Cause and Effect</u> and <u>Mind Reading</u> <u>Patterns</u>:

Step 1: Listen to the client's Surface Structure;

Step 2: Determine if it involves (a) a claim that one person is performing some action which causes another person to experience some emotion or (b) a claim that one person comes to know what another person is thinking and feeling;

Step 3: Respond by asking, how, specifically, these processes occur.

PRESUPPOSITIONS

Presuppositions are one linguistic reflex of the process of Distortion. The purpose in recognizing presuppositions is to assist the client in identifying those basic assumptions which impoverish his/her model and limit his/her options for coping. Linguistically, these basic assumptions show up as presuppositions of the person's Surface Structure. For example, to make sense out of the Surface Structure,

"I'm afraid that my son is turning out to be as lazy as my husband,"

you have to accept as true the situation expressed by the sentence presupposed by this sentence,

"My husband is lazy."

Notice that this last Surface Structure (the presupposition of the one before), does not appear directly as any part of the sentence which presupposes it. Linguists have developed a test for determining what the presuppositions of any given sentence are. (Adapted for the Meta Model):

Step-by-step for determining presuppositions:

Step 1: Listen for the <u>main process word or verb</u> in the person's Surface Structure - call this sentence A.

Step 2: Create a new Surface Structure by introducing the negative word in the person's original Surface Structure on the main verb - call this sentence B.

Step 3: Ask yourself what must be true for both A and B to make sense.

Step 4: Ask the client to explore or accept the presupposition and ask the client to specify the verb and replace the deleted material. Example: "I'm afraid that my son is turning out to be as lazy as my husband."

By introducing the negative of the main verb (afraid), you create a second sentence,

"I'm not afraid that my son is turning out to be as lazy as my husband."

The point here is that for you to make sense out of this new Surface Structure it must be true that,

"My husband is lazy."

Since both the person's original Surface Structure and the new Surface Structure formed from it by introducing the negative element require that this last sentence be true, this last Surface Structure is the presupposition of the client's original sentence.

META MODEL WORKSHEET III

Directions: Write an appropriate challenge for each Meta model pattern described.

Mind Reading: The belief on the part of the speaker that one person can know what the other person is thinking/feeling without a direct communication on the part of the other person.

1. It's too bad that you don't like the way that I act.

_____

2. I'm sure they liked your presentation.

_____

3. I know what makes her happy.

_____

4. Believe me, I know what's best for you.

_____

<u>**Cause and Effect**</u>: Involves the belief on the part of the speaker that one person (or set of circumstances) may perform some action which necessarily causes some emotion or internal state.

1. My spouse really makes me feel angry.

    _____

2. Her behavior forced me to feel incredibly incompetent.

    _____

3. Your ideas/attitudes annoy/irritate me.

    _____

4. His plan insults me.

    _____

Presuppositions: What within the structure of the sentence must be true in order for the whole sentence to be true. On this set also list what must be true in addition to writing a challenge.

1.   If she does it again, I'll leave her.

   _____

   _____

2.   People keep dumping more responsibility on my shoulders.

   _____

   _____

3.   His poor appearance doesn't reflect the company image.

   _____

   _____

4.   It was her nasty attitude that made me fire her.

   _____

   _____

HYPNOTIC LANGUAGE PATTERNS: THE MILTON MODEL

Milton Erickson used language very systematically in his hypnotic work, often in unusual ways. These patterns were first described by Bandler and Grinder in their book, Patterns of Hypnotic Techniques of Milton H. Erickson, M.D., Vol. 1.

Using this "**Milton Model**" is a prerequisite to effective hypnotic communication, and of the induction examples in this book. Many readers will unconsciously begin to learn the hypnotic language patterns by reading the many examples of inductions in this book. This appendix makes these patterns more explicit, so that you can practice using one pattern at a time in order to systematically incorporate them all into your behavior. Many effective communicators use these language patterns to enhance their persuasion and influencing skills, while respecting another's model of the world.

I.   Inverse Meta Model Patterns

Often the Milton Model has been called the reverse of the Meta Model. The Meta Model is described fully in, The Structure of Magic, Vol I, by Bandler and Grinder, and there is an excellent 12-page summary of it in an appendix to, They Lived Happily Ever After, by Leslie Cameron-Bandler. The Meta Model is a set of language patterns that can be used to specify experience more fully. In contrast, the Milton Model provides the user with ways of being "**artfully vague.**" Being artfully vague allows a communicator to make statements that sound specific and yet are general enough to be an adequate pace for the listener's experience, no matter what that is. The Meta Model provides ways of recovering specific information that is deleted in any sentence; the Milton Model provides ways of constructing sentences in which almost all specific information is deleted. This requires the listener to fill in the deletions from his/her own unique internal experience. The Inverse Meta Model can also be conveniently divided into three chunks: Gathering Information; Semantic Ill-formedness; and Limits of the Speaker's Model.

A.   Gathering Information

A part of the Milton Model is called **Deleting Information,** and is the most useful of the three chunks for hypnotic purposes. The four sub-categories follow.

1.   **Nominalizations:** Nominalizations are words that take the place of a noun in a sentence, but they are not tangible - they cannot be touched, felt, or heard. The test for a nominalization is "Can you put it in a wheelbarrow?" If a word is a noun and it cannot be put in a wheelbarrow, it is a nominalization. Words like *curiosity, hypnosis, learnings, love*, etc. are nominalizations. They are used as nouns, but they are actually process words.

Whenever a nominalization is used, much information is deleted. If I say, "Emily has a lot of knowledge," I've deleted what exactly she knows and how she knows it. Nominalizations are very effective in hypnotic inductions because they allow the speaker to be vague and require the listener to search through her experience for the most appropriate meaning. Milton Erickson's inductions are filled with them.

In the following example, the nominalizations are in italics: "I know that you have a certain *difficulty* in your *life* that you would like to bring to a satisfactory *resolution*. . .and I'm not sure exactly what personal *resources* you would find most useful in resolving this *difficulty*, but I do know that your *unconscious mind* is better able than you to search through your *experience* for exactly that *resource* .."

In this paragraph nothing specific is mentioned, but if this kind of statement is made to a client who has come in to resolve a problem, she will provide specific personal meanings for the nominalizations used. By using nominalizations the hypnotist can provide useful instructions without running the risk of saying something that runs counter to the listener's internal experience.

2. **Unspecified Verbs:** No verb is completely specified, but verbs can be more or less specified. If a hypnotist uses relatively unspecified verbs, the listener is again forced to supply the meaning in order to understand the sentence. Words like *do, fix, solve, move, change, wonder, think, sense, know, experience, understand, remember, become aware of*, etc., are relatively unspecified.

The sentence "I *think* this is true" is less specified than " I *feel* this is true." In the latter sentence, we are informed as to how the person thinks. If I say, "I want you to *learn*," I am using a very unspecified verb, since I'm not explaining how I want you to learn, or what specifically I want you to learn about what.

3. **Unspecified Referential Index:** This means that the noun being talked about is not specified.

> "*People* can relax."
> "*This* can be easily learned."
> "You can notice a *certain sensation*."

Statements like these give the listener the opportunity to easily apply the sentence to themselves in order to understand it.

B.   Semantic Ill-formedness

1. **Causal Modeling, or Linkage** Using words that imply a cause-effect relationship between something that is occurring and something the communicator wants to occur invites the listener to respond as if one thing did indeed "cause" the other. There are three kinds of linkage, with varying degrees of strength.

    a.   The weakest kind of linkage makes use of conjunctions to connect otherwise unrelated phenomena: "You are listening to the sound of my voice, *and* you can begin to relax;" "You are breathing in and out *and* you are curious about what you might learn."

b.   The second kind of linkage makes use of words like *as, when, during,* and *while* to connect statements by establishing a connection in time: "*As* you sit there smiling, you can begin to go into a trance;" "*While* you sway back and forth, you can relax more completely."

c.   The third and strongest kind of linkage uses words actually stating causality. Words such as *makes, causes, forces,* and *requires* can be used: "The nodding of your head will *make* you relax more completely."

Notice that when using each kind of linkage, the communicator begins with something that is already occurring and connects to it something she wants to occur. The communicator will be most effective if she begins with the weakest form of linkage and gradually moves to a stronger form.

These forms of linkage work by implying or stating that what is occurring will cause something else to occur, and by making a gradual transition for the listener between what is occurring and some other experience.

2.   **Mind Reading.** Acting as if you know the internal experience of another person can be an effective tool to build the credibility of the hypnotist as long as the mind reading makes use of generalized language patterns. If the mind reading is too specific, the communicator runs the risk of saying something counter to the listener's experience, and thereby losing rapport: "You may be wondering what I'll say next;" "You're curious about hypnosis."

3.   **Lost Performative.** Evaluative statements in which the person making the evaluation is missing (lost) from the sentence are called Lost Performatives. Statements using lost performatives can be an effective way of delivering presuppositions: "It's good that you can relax so easily;" "It's not important that you sink all the way down in your chair."

C. Limits of the Speaker's Model

This chunk of the Meta Model is the least significant chunk as a part of the Milton Model. Its two categories can be used to limit the listener's model in ways that produce trance as well as other outcomes.

1. **Universal Quantifiers.** Words such as *all, every, always, never, nobody,* etc., are universal quantifiers. These words usually indicate overgeneralization. "And now you can go *all* the way into a trance;" "*Every* thought that you have can assist you in going deeper into a trance."

2. **Modal Operators.** Words such as *should, must, have to, can't, won't,* etc., that indicate lack of choice: "Have you noticed that you *can't* open your eyes?"

There are several other Milton Model Language Patterns which you can read about in the books listed above and practice in "NLP and Ericksonian Hypnosis" Seminars.

RAPPORT

THE IMPORTANCE OF RAPPORT

A lot of information needs to be exchanged between people daily. We have minutes and hours, not years, to spend with the people who support our business and our personal lives. The ability to gather and/or exchange information effectively saves us time, energy and consequently money.

Numerous studies and reports have documented that one necessary skill in exchanging information effectively is the ability to build rapport. Building rapport allows you to gather needed information graciously and expediently. Rapport means responsiveness, not that you like and/or agree with someone. There is a difference between giving people the experience of being understood and regarded, and actually understanding what their communication means. We are currently talking about providing people with the experience of being understood and regarded.

You are already familiar with "macro" types of mirroring in your ongoing experience. An example of mirroring on this scale is dressing appropriately for a particular occasion. As a more refined example, we tend to match our table manners and body postures to the level of formality we perceive to be congruent with the place and people with whom we are dining. Mirroring on its various levels is the behavioral equivalent of agreeing with someone verbally.

BEHAVIORS YOU CAN MIRROR:

I.   BODY MIRRORING

Body Posture
Hand Gestures
Facial Expressions
Weight Shifts
Breathing
Movement of Feet
Eye Movements

II.   VOCAL/VERBAL MIRRORING

Tempo of Speech
Volume of Speech
Auditory Tone
Highly Valued Descriptors
Predicates

To begin learning how to mirror, take the time to watch other people interact. Watch children playing; observe folks in restaurants, meetings, and cocktail parties. Anytime you are near people who are interacting, notice how much mirroring is going on. Also, notice the quality of interaction that occurs when mirroring is absent.

After a short period of time in an observer's position, you will know that people instinctively mirror each other. You can now begin to do so deliberately to achieve specific outcomes (which we will discuss later). Start by mirroring just one aspect of another person's behavior while talking to them. When this is easy, add another discreet piece - like their voice tempo - and another, and then another, until you are mirroring without thinking about it, but can consistently observe it in your behavior in retrospect.

The more you practice, the more aware you will become of the rhythms that you and others generate with gestures and breathing patterns, and in voice tones, tempo and intonation patterns. Be sure to notice the degree to which people are out of sync when they are miscommunicating, in contrast to how they are in sync when doing well with one another. When mirroring to establish rapport, be sure to <u>be subtle</u>.

Though mirroring might feel awkward to the novice, its value in achieving and maintaining rapport makes it worth doing whatever is necessary to become skilled. It requires effort to learn how to mirror effectively. You need to tune your attention to portions of your own and others' actions of which you were previously unaware. Mirroring is something we automatically do. We are talking here about <u>mirroring purposely</u> in order <u>to build rapport toward a desired goal or outcome</u>.

RAPPORT - THE STRUCTURE OF MATCHING

Pacing is the process by which you can establish and maintain rapport. Pacing is simply the process of moving as the other person moves. Pacing emphasizes the importance of acknowledging aspects of the other person's behavior, thereby meeting the other person at their model of the world. You simply utilize the other person's own behavior to establish and maintain rapport. Pacing begins by recognizing that people are always communicating and do so in systematic ways. Therefore, anything you can identify you can pace, by adjusting your own behavior (non-verbal and verbal) to move with the other person.

The purpose of this list is to offer you a variety of ways to establish rapport in a meaningful way. The outcome of mastering the art of pacing will be the ability to establish rapport with whoever you choose. It is extremely important to be graceful and respectful in your pacing so that what you are doing does not come into the conscious awareness of the other person.

WHOLE BODY MATCHING - adjust your body to approximate the other person's stance.

HALF BODY MATCHING - Match the upper or lower portion of the other person's body.

HEAD/SHOULDERS ANGLE - Match characteristic poses that the person offers with their head and/or shoulders.

FACIAL EXPRESSIONS - Note the ways the person uses their face, e.g., wrinkles their nose, purses their lips, raises their eyebrows, etc.

GESTURES - With minute and graceful movements of your own match those gestures of the other person.

PART BODY MATCHING - Pacing any consistent stylistic use of the body, e.g., eye blinks.

VOCAL QUALITIES - Match tonality, tempo, volume, intensity, timbre, etc.

REPRESENTATIONAL SYSTEMS - Detect and use (by matching) in your own language the primary predicates of the other person.

REPETITIVE PHRASING - Note and match in your own language the repeated phrases of the other person.

BREATHING - Adjust your own breathing to be in sync with the other person's breathing.

CROSS OVER MATCHING (MIRRORING) - Using one aspect of your behavior to match a different aspect of the other person's behavior, e.g., adjusting your voice tempo to match the rhythm of a person's breathing; pacing their eye blinks with your finger or head nods; pacing their voice tempo with your head nods or breathing, etc.

MATCHING AND MISMATCHING - EFFECTS ON RAPPORT

PURPOSE: To demonstrate the effects on rapport when matching or mismatching predicates and posture.

1. While engaged in conversations with family members and business colleagues select a specific behavior to place your attention on and match. You might select one behavior per day to practice. Remember to practice mismatching also and be sure to end the interaction in a state of rapport. What are some contexts where you may want to end the interaction with mismatching?

2. Some methods for consideration:

    Match posture and predicates

    Match posture and mismatch predicates

    Match predicates and mismatch posture

    Mismatch posture and predicates

    Match tone and tempo

    Match tempo only

    Match tempo and volume

    Match physically and mismatch vocally

    Match vocally and mismatch physically

    Match physically and vocally

HOW TO DEVELOP THE ART OF PERSUASION

To the extent that you can "match" another person's behavior, both verbally and non-verbally, you will be pacing that person's experience. Mirroring, or matching, a technique used to achieve rapport, is the process of building trust; and there are as many dimensions to it as your sensory experience can discern. You can mirror/match the other person's predicates, syntax, body posture, breathing, voice tonality and tempo, expressions, facial mannerisms (such as eye blinks), and many other facets of the person's behavior. The other person can be completely unconscious of your mirroring, and it will still have a profound effect on him/her.

There are two types of non-verbal pacing (or mirroring):

1.   **Direct Mirroring**

> Example: Breathing at the same rate and depth as the other person.

2.   **Cross over Mirroring**

> (Substituting one non-verbal channel for another)

> a.   Cross-over the same channel

> > Example: Using your hand movement to pace the other person's breathing movement (kinesthetic channel).

> b.   Cross-over by using a different channel

> > Example: Matching your voice tempo (auditory) to the other person's rate of breathing (kinesthetic).

It is important to have a choice between direct mirroring and/or cross-over mirroring. With someone who breathes normally, pace them directly with your breathing (direct mirroring). With an asthmatic, pace with your hand movement or anything else (cross-over mirroring) certainly not your own breathing!

Some people feel like they just have to mirror. This is referred to as compulsive mirroring. If you believe that you must have empathy for another person, often this means that you have to have the same feelings that they have in order for you to communicate effectively. If you have to understand their experience by actually experiencing it, then you're potentially in for some unpleasant feelings.

A young woman who was an exceptionally effective communicator, and who mirrored rather compulsively, attended a regional sales seminar for her organization. As she was conversing with a fellow participant (and mirroring as she normally did in her conversations), she began sliding down in her chair in much the same manner as her conversationalist was. One slide too many, and the young woman literally fell on the floor! Her conversationalist, conscious of his mirroring, remained in his chair.

*****

A young attorney walked into his office rather late one morning, saying to his secretary (who felt she just had to mirror), "You know, I have this phobia everytime I get on a crowded elevator . . . I feel like I'm going to throw up . . . I start getting this nauseous feeling in my stomach and I get light-headed . . . like I'm swaying . . . you know what I mean?"

The new secretary promptly excused herself and ran for the nearest ladies' room!

BEWARE OF COMPULSIVE MIRRORING!

*****

PACING AND LEADING

Pacing is the term used to describe purposeful repetitive matching. Any of the behaviors listed on "The Importance of Rapport" handout can be paced. The primary purpose of pacing is to build rapport.

Leading is done to <u>test rapport</u> or <u>elicit a desired state</u>. In order to lead you select a specific behavior you have been pacing (e.g. auditory volume) and then you increase or decrease your behavior (e.g., increase or decrease the volume). When someone responds by following you (e.g., increasing or decreasing their volume) <u>within 30 to 90 seconds</u> a successful lead has been accomplished. If your outcome for leading is to test rapport and the individual follows you, now is the time to gather or present information. When your outcome is to elicit a desired state and the individual follows your lead, you continue pacing and leading until you can see and hear external cues indicating the desired state is present.

Pacing and leading is a pattern that is evident in almost everything that we do and, most of the time we are not consciously aware of when we're doing it. Here again lies the difference between those people who can lead other people into new behavior (or action) and those who do not. If pacing and leading is done gracefully, it will work with anyone! Pacing, in essence, is sharing the other person's behavioral reality - and what automatically develops as a result of graceful pacing is rapport and trust with the other person. The important factor in pacing is the choice you have of going from one reality to another and still maintaining the appropriate perspective for each reality. A successful communicator will alter his/her behavior to reflect his/her surroundings and maintain his/her perspective for each reality. This is what is commonly referred to as "changing hats." The only time pacing should not be used is if you are trying to (1) decrease rapport or (2) decrease credibility. Leading, however evokes a change in the other person's behavior - creating action which will give you the outcome you want. Pacing and leading work hand-in-hand. Without the ability to lead the other person into new behavior (action), pacing might necessarily be ineffective in producing the outcome you want. You must know your outcome in order to know when to pace and when to lead the person. There are well-formedness conditions for outcomes which can be learned, thereby enhancing your persuasion skills.

Four stages occur in the pacing process:

1.   Matching the state the other person is experiencing;

2.   Pacing the individual;

3.   Selecting the behavior to lead;

4   Gently leading him/her to test rapport or elicit a desired state.

MATCHING

Please circle the letter of the response that you might make to match the representational systems used in the original sentence.

1.   Everything is dim. I want to see what's ahead more clearly.

   a.   Let's clear away the fog so you can come to grips with your situation.

   b.   Sounds like there's too much haze. You can't hear yourself think.

   c.   I want to assist you in shining some light on your future.

   d.   Yes, I understand. And what's more important are the feelings behind the dimness.

2.   I can't get in touch with what you're saying.

   a.   Let me say it more clearly.

   b.   Let me say it another way so you can get a handle on it.

   c.   Could you grasp it if I painted it a bit more clearly?

   d.   What specifically can't you understand?

3.   I can't seem to focus on my feelings.

   a.   What stops you from getting a handle on them?

   b.   What feelings can't you tune in to?

   c.   How would they look to you if you had a handle on them?

   d.   What would happen if you could come to grips with them?

4. I get too much static from my partners.

   a. Noisy people, aren't they?

   b. How are they cramping your style?

   c. How do they make you feel uncomfortable?

   d. You feel that they are upset with you.

5. The warmth is gone from our relationship.

   a. What would brighten up your relationship?

   b. So, you'd like to relate in better ways.

   c. What do you think would bring the harmony back into your relationship?

   d. How would you like to rekindle the fire?

6. What is the structure of the basic pattern for establishing rapport?

7. How do you know when you're in rapport with another person?

8. Give an example of "Cross-Over Mirroring" and a context in which you would consider it more appropriate than direct mirroring.

ANSWERS: 1.c, 2.b, 3.c, 4.a, 5.d

OUTCOMES

FRAMING

Framing is the process we use to select, delete and arrange what we are thinking about. Framing refers to how we make meaning out of something. A frame can be described as a mental pattern or map or template that enables us to make sense of something. If two people have the same mental map or frame of reference, they will be more likely to put the same meaning on an event or fact, and this similarity will be reflected in their output or behavior. But if one person's frame of reference is different, the meaning that person makes will be different. If a person has no map or frame, no meaning can be made. The inputs just will not compute. When we make meaning out of something, we select and arrange the way we see reality. In accordance with the frame we are using, we select what inputs to pay attention to, and what outputs are useful or relevant to produce. We always use some frame when we think.

Through the modeling of effective communicators in the professions of psychotherapy and business, Bandler and Grinder developed a set of frames based on a guiding model of knowing the present state, defining the desired state (the situation to be achieved), and developing strategies to move in the desired direction. The frames or contexts are established for economy of movement and to set appropriate boundary conditions on information relevant to the task. Frames or contexts provide focus or an explicit way of sorting the appropriate out of the myriad options potentially available. Frames or contexts may, for example, gather resources for a common starting point or expand boundaries which are too restrictive for a particular outcome. Frames or contexts may access resources which even the holder was not aware he or she had. Grinder, McMaster (1980)

1. **Outcome Frame**: a description of the state the person desires to achieve at the end of a particular communication. It specifies which comments or contributions, which experiences or resources, are appropriate in the context of that particular communication or meeting. Once the outcome is well-defined you would want to use Relevancy Challenges (a Precision Procedure covered in more detail in the Meeting section of your manual).

2. **Backtrack Frame**: a verbal and nonverbal recapitulation of the information elicited in the immediately preceding portion of the discussion (since the last Backtrack Frame). The primary purpose of the Backtrack Frame is to refresh the participants' memory or to establish for new members the track the discussion has taken up to that point and to secure their agreement with important information that has been brought to light. It can be used as a technique for building/maintaining rapport (pacing) by feeding back what someone has just said and done.

3. **"As If" Frame**: a way to make it possible to elicit the information and/or behavior required for the Desired State to be reached as effectively as possible, given the present resources of the individual or group, which could otherwise be unavailable. This includes the assignment of roles or characteristics to various members of groups or the creating and establishing of information contrary to fact which shifts the context in which the group/individual is operating to one where the information or behavior required is made available.

This frame was established after modeling Milton Erickson's use of a trance technique called **Pseudo-Orientation in Time**. After a client was in the appropriate altered state Dr. Erickson would disorient him/her from the present. "Today is October 8. But a week ago, you could have looked forward a week to October 8, wondering what you would do between now and then. And the day that then was now, is now then. A month later than that you can look back on the events of the past month and see how your plans turned out, but two months before that, you might have been just getting ready to make those plans," etc. Orient the person to 6 months from now. "Now it's April, 1987. You may remember back in October that you came to see me about a problem of great importance that was troubling you at that time. If you think back on that time, the problem seems far away, particularly since you've now solved that problem to your total satisfaction, and you have all the changes you want. Tell me what it is like for you now, now that that situation is no longer a problem." This technique can get the same kind of effect in the "waking state." Then we call it the "As If" Frame.

4. **Ecology Frame**: Changing or expanding the frame to be sure that the proposed change or new behavior is also good for the whole system: person, family, business organization, etc.

OUTCOME

Outcome - the result that you want to achieve in a given situation.

1. **Desired State** - a desired state is an organization of internal and external behaviors and responses that represents the experience of an outcome.

2. **Well-Formedness Conditions**

    •   Stated in Positives

    •   Evidence Procedure

    •   Specified and Contextualized

    •   Initiated and Maintained by the Individual

    •   Ecological

3. **Present State**- Present state is the organization of internal and external behaviors and responses that generates what is experienced as a problem.

OUTCOMES

Communicating without a desired outcome is like traveling without a destination. You may end up in a place you really enjoy, or you may not. Enjoying your trip is a perfectly good outcome; ending up at the destination you want is also productive.

An outcome is the result you want, defined in terms of the way you would like to see things happen, the way you want to feel, and what you will hear when you have your outcome. Most business people already know about goal-setting and management by objectives. You may have placed the word outcome in the same category. But goals and objectives are in a broader category than outcomes. Outcomes are goals that have been clarified and finely honed by the use of the well-formedness conditions. In other words, if goals and objectives are like new pencils just out of a box, outcomes are like sharpened pencils that are ready to do what you want.

The study of outcomes is divided into three areas:

1. Desired State or Situation

2. Well-Formedness Conditions

3. Present State or Situation

---

1. Desired State or Situation

A Desired State is an organization of internal and external behaviors and responses that represent the experience of an outcome. It is the final representation of a strategy that worked elegantly in getting that outcome. It is characterized by outcome thinking. In **outcome thinking** you focus on what you are moving toward, rather than something you are moving away from. Remember that whenever someone starts talking and/or thinking about what they want they are giving you external cues (nonverbal and vocal) which you can calibrate and consequently recognize in the future as being the desired state. Internal states always have a corresponding external state.

2. Well-Formedness Conditions

The behavioral information you learn to detect assures that you are responding to sensory information rather than to your own interpretations, and protects the client from being cured of your problems. However, when you attend to such behavioral information, there is an overwhelming quantity of it presented with each interaction. For it to be useful to you and to the communication process, it is necessary to establish a specific outcome to work toward. This reduces the complexity by providing a guideline for determining the relevancy of the verbal and non-verbal information you are perceiving. Establishing a specific outcome is the prerequisite for being able to answer the recurring question, "Is this pertinent to what we are working to achieve?" It keeps you from having to respond to every incongruity, accessing cue, Meta-Model violation, etc., and focuses your efforts in a purposeful way toward the agreed-upon goal. Having clearly stated outcomes also provides both you and your client with a means to evaluate progress.

There are five conditions that must be met for an outcome to be well-formed:

- Stated in the Positive.

- Demonstrated in Sensory Experience - provides an Evidence Procedure.

- Appropriately Specified and Contextualized.

- Initiated and Maintained by the Individual - within their Control.

- Ecological - maintains the homeostasis of the system.

First, the outcome must be **stated in the positive**. Find out what someone does want, not what is unwanted. If you were helping someone arrange furniture and they said to you, "I don't want that chair there," you would not have the information to know what to do with the chair or what to put in its place. Like the person who doesn't like the position of the chair, often clients, family members and/or employees know what they don't want. For example, a job applicant telling you that she/he doesn't want to work on weekends, or an employee stating they do not like the way a particular display is set up. Some possible questions/comments for these, with the purpose of finding out what the individual wants, are: What would be the ideal work schedule for you?; What is an acceptable work schedule?; I'm curious, how would you arrange the display; What changes to the display could be made to make it attractive?

A **second** criterion for a well-formed outcome is that it be **demonstrable in sensory experience** to both you and the person you are communicating with. Insights can be enlightening and useful but they do not constitute an experiential change. What would you and those you communicate with need to **see**, **hear**, and/or **feel** in order to know that you have accomplished your outcome, is the question to be answered: e.g.; if you and your family decided to have a meeting to plan a vacation what would be your evidence you had succeeded? Would you have a location selected? Would it be written down? Would the details for making arrangements be delegated to specific family members? It is imperative to determine mutually satisfying **evidence procedures**. Success can not be recognized unless we know when we have achieved our goal.

The **third** well-formedness condition is that the outcome be **appropriately contextualized and specified**. In what contexts do you want it? In what contexts do you not want it? When, where, with whom do you want it? If an employee tells you they think they deserve a raise and you agree, the appropriate next step is to determine specifically how much of a raise, the date the raise is effective, and the criteria each of you used to come to this conclusion.

The **fourth** condition which must be met for an outcome to be well-formed is that the outcome be one that can be **initiated and maintained by the individual**. For example, one function of a manager is to assist employees in having choices over their own experience so that their well-being can be maintained through time without the need for the manager's (or anyone else's) continued assistance. People often ask for a change in someone else's behavior - "If customers would state more specifically what they want," or "be more responsible," or "be more considerate," "then I would be more friendly and eager to assist." While this is genuinely the individual's experience, to assist them in achieving that outcome further reinforces the belief that their work experience is dependent on the behavior of others.

For an experience or behavior to be initiated and maintained by an individual assumes that he/she has the means to achieve the experience or behavior on their own. One possibility is to assist the employee in the above example by inviting them to remember other times in their life when they chose to be friendly toward people in spite of how folks were acting. Once they recall some times, regardless of how long ago, where, or with whom, you can ask them what they did then and whether or not they think that behavior might assist them now with the customer(s) with whom they were experiencing difficulty.

The fifth well-formedness condition is to **preserve ecology**. By definition, ecology is the branch of biology that deals with the relations between living organisms and their enviornments. In relation to human behavior and outcomes, we use the term to remind us that in order for a goal to be achieved the outcomes must fit into the totality of our lives and preserve a balance. If a manager fills a particular position to have flexible work hours and the potential applicant is bound by certain time constraints (taking classes at a local university, etc.) our outcome may not be able to be obtained and preserve the well-being of that applicant. Questions like, "what resources, skills do you need to get this outcome?," or "what is the first step you can take now, toward your outcome?," or "what prevents you from getting your outcome?," assist in preserving ecology.

Questions for Elicitation of a Well-Formed Outcome:

1.   Stated in the Positive

- What do I/we want?

2.   Demonstrated in Sensory Experience

- What would be my evidence that I had achieved my outcome?

- How would you know if you were getting your outcome?

- What would you be doing to get it?

  - EB - External Behavior - what would you be seeing and hearing?

  - IS - Internal State - what would be feeling?

  - IP - Internal Processing - how would you represent this?

- What would be a demonstration of it? (remember you get to see the external behavior here)

3. **Appropriately Specified and Contextualized**

    *   Where do I/we want this outcome?

    *   Where do I/we not want this outcome?

    *   When do I/we want this outcome?

    *   When do I/we not want this outcome?

    *   With whom do I/we want this outcome?

    *   With whom do I/we not want this outcome?

4. **Initiated and Maintained by the Individual**

    *   What resources can I/we activate to get this outcome?

    *   What resources can I/we acquire to get this outcome?

    *   What can I/we do?

    *   What can I/we begin to do today?

    *   What can I/we continue doing?

5. **Ecological**

    *   What would happen if I/we got this outcome?

    *   How will getting this outcome affect other aspects of my/our life?

    *   How does getting this outcome benefit me/us?

    *   Is the positive by-product preserved? (see reframing section)

OUTCOME FRAMING EXERCISE: DESIRED STATE OR SITUATION

Determine which of the following outcomes are well formed. For those that are not, identify the well-formedness condition(s) that are violated. Then rewrite the outcome so that it is a well formed outcome.

1. I want to have a set of key words and phrases for each of my five major clients that represents what they value most in my service/product.

   _____

   _____

2. Our department needs to develop better interpersonal communication skills.

   _____

   _____

3. I want to be able to motivate my subordinates.

   _____

   _____

4.   I want to avoid inefficient business practices.

_____

_____

5.   I want each of my sales poeple to act as if they were independent entrepreneurs.

_____

_____

6.   I want to be a better listener.

_____

_____

7.   I want to be able to verbally intimidate my subordinates by yelling at them when they don't keep up with scheduled reports.

_____

_____

8.   I want to be able to motivate myself.

_____

_____

9.   I want my children to be honest.

_____

_____

10.   I want our monthly staff meetings to be characterized by creative input from all attending.

_____

_____

11.   I want my wife to show me she loves me by sending me a friendship card once a month to my office.

_____

_____

12.   Meetings should not waste the time of top managers.

_____

_____

```
FORMING A USEFUL OUTCOME - OUTLINE
              OF
   DESIRED STATE OR SITUATION
```

- Problem Statement:

- Outcome Statement:

- Evidence Procedure:

- Specified and Contextualized:

- Initiated and Maintained by You:

- Ecological:

- First Step:

DESIRED STATE OR SITUATION
CHUNKING DOWN WORKSHEET

This exercise will help you to learn the process for chunking your outcome down to a size you can manage. Select a problem or issue from your earlier discussion. Take turns working with your partner on one problem at a time, to chunk it down to a size you can handle.

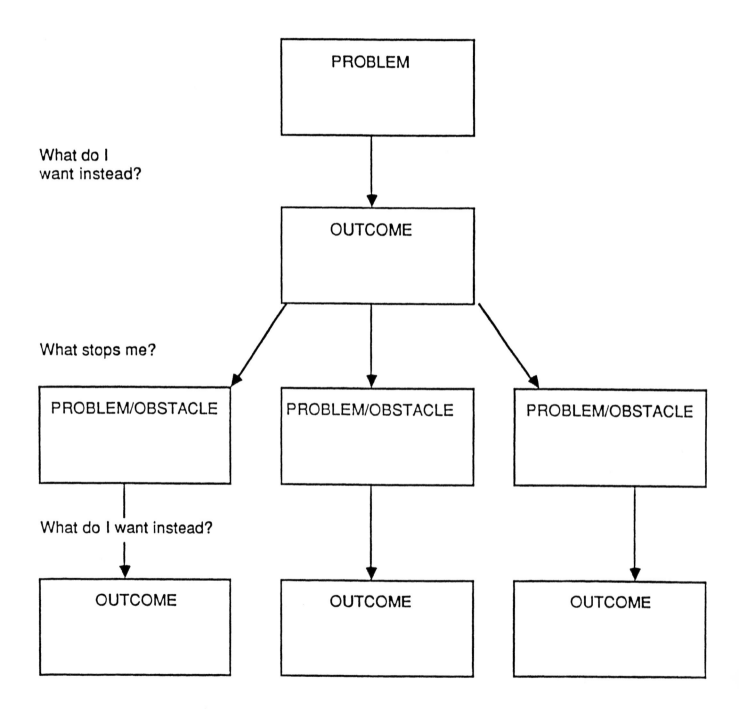

ENLARGING THE FRAME (CHUNKING UP)

What are my alternatives?

1.

2.

3.

CHUNK DOWN

What is my first step?

I. S. that requires relief or satisfaction.

CHUNK UP

CHUNK UP

FLIP

STUCK

I have alternatives
and I can move.

What would that
do for me?

If I got that, what would
that do for me?

What do I want instead?

Obstacle in a small frame.

3. Present State

Present state is the organization of internal and external behaviors and responses experienced as a problem. The present state/problem state represents a strategy that works elegantly in getting that person's problem. It is usually more efficient to elicit the present state after you have elicited a well-formed desired state outcome (once you have the outcome you can keep people on the track by using the relevancy challenge in relation to the outcome, e.g., how is talking about X relevant, given the outcome?) It is essential for the person's ecology that you find out how having this problem is benefitting them, how it is serving them; would they be deprived by not having this problem, etc., in order to preserve positive-by-product secondary gains. Present state is usually characterized by problem thinking. In problem thinking energy is focused in analyzing what's wrong, history, background, and even blame.

People will ask questions and/or tell you about:

- What caused this problem: Why do you have it?

- Who is to blame for this problem?

- Who else is experiencing the effects of this problem?

- What roadblocks or barriers do you see in solving this problem?

- What other problems is this problem causing?

Problem thinking like this generally results in low energy, wasted time, discouragement and being stuck.

Questions for Eliciting Present/Problem State Frame:

- What stops you from getting your outcome? (This question will usually put the person into the present state - remember to calibrate so you will recognize if you see it again.)

- What in the external and/or internal environment lets the person know to go into this specific present state? Sensory-based description of the external and/or internal trigger.

- What mental strategy does the person engage in? Images, sounds, words, feelings, sensations, etc. Some may be conscious, and/or unconscious - watch/listen for repeated and consistent physiological accessing cues, e.g., eye movements, change in breathing, gestures, tonal shifts, etc., as well as listen to the word(s). Two or three steps are usually sufficient.

- What is the person conscious of? This may be one or two of the above steps.

- What is the person's external behavior? Sensory based description - calibrate so you will recognize it if you see it again.

- What is the sequence of the above information?

- What is the positive by-product (if any) of having this problem? If there is a positive by-product, it must be included in the well-formedness conditions of the outcome.

Possible Present State Questions:

1. How do you know X is a problem? (internal processes and/or what is consciously represented)

2. How do you know when to have X? (trigger)

3. When/with whom does X work for you/is X useful? (positive by-product)

THE BACKTRACK FRAME

Definition: A verbal and nonverbal recapitulation of the information elicited in the immediately preceding portion of the discussion, since the last Backtrack Frame.

Purposes:

- to review prior information, discussions, etc.

- to update new participants.

- to secure agreement on information up to this point.

- to open a meeting.

Uses:

- provides precise understanding that a transaction has occurred.

- provides summary and prevents losing track of the desired outcome.

- rechecks that all parties involved are in agreement on the information exchanged thus far.

- builds/maintains rapport.

THE "AS IF" FRAME

Purpose: To establish a context contrary to the fact or Frame in which the desired information or behavior becomes available. It is appropriate whenever the communicator determines that there is a condition in the actual present situation which is blocking access to information or behavior which moves toward the intended Desired State.

Steps:

Establish the Frame - Use the following lead-in words and phrase:

- Let's suppose that. . . . .

- If you were to. . . . .

- Can you act as if. . . . .

- Pretend that I am. . . . .

Decide on Type:

- Person Switch - If you were me, what. . . . .

- Time Switch - Act as if it was six months down the road. . . . .

- Function Switch - If you could change any part of the operation .

- Information Switch - Let's suppose we had that information. . . . .

Uses:

1. When something in the actual present situation is blocking access to information or behavior which leads to intended goal. You hear the assertion that needed information or behavior is unavailable. Ask, "What if _____ were available or possible?"

2. When you want to go into the future as though the person already had their outcome, in order to do a final check. You hear that the individual can not be sure about _____ until some later time. Ask, "If it were _____ from now, then what would you think?"

3. When a staff/family member is absent from a meeting and their information is necessary in order to continue the current discussion. You hear someone say, "Sam has that information and he wasn't able to come today." Ask, "If Sam was here, what do you think he'd report?"

ECOLOGY FRAME

Checking for ecology is reframing, in the sense that you change or expand the frame to be sure that the proposed change or new behavior is also good for the whole system: person, family, business organization, etc.

Ongoing Ecology Check:

1.   Watch and listen for incongruent responses as the person describes the desired outcome.

2.   Start with the assumption that the person doesn't have what he/she wants because there are good reasons for him/her not to have it, and that giving it to them is a sure way to harm him/her. (Be prepared to give up this assumption only after you have checked it out thoroughly.)

3.   Ask yourself, "What problems could be caused by the proposed change? Will it get only the outcome that is wanted? What will be lost by having X behavior?" (There will always be a loss, though it may be trivial.) Check out anything you think could be a problem.

Ways to Check for Ecology:

•   Future-pace in all relevant contexts. Watch for incongruence. Ask, "As you try out these behaviors in your imagination, notice what you will lose if you get this new behavioral choice?;" or "Is there anything you don't like about the new choice?"

•   Check for anything the client deletes. Does the client consider the internal responses, internal computations, and external behaviors of all other relevant people with respect to the proposed change?

- "What stops you from having the change now?" "What stopped you in the past?" ('past-pacing')

- Have them role-play the new behavior and judge how it could be a problem.

- Have them switch referential index and play other people responding to the change.

- To press for a response, play polarity: "Oh, how wonderful this will be ! -- no problems at all. . ." or "I know there are problems and I won't proceed to give you this choice until you've identified them all."

- Use transderivational search pattern to find out other contexts that this state is active in, and examine how it functions there. (How does this person generalize this outcome or behavior to other contexts?) How can you limit the outcome to only those contexts where it is useful?

- Assume that every behavior/response either: a) has a positive/function intent, or b) is a by-product of a function. If a problem is only a by-product, you can probably change it with relatively few unecological consequences. If the problem has a function, the desired outcome must satisfy the same function to avoid unecological consequences. For example, if the client asks for relief from anxiety, the feelings of anxiety could be a by-product of how he/she plans, or it could have the function of motivating him/her. If the anxiety motivates, then the desired behavior must include the function of motivation.

- When a person asks for something, examine the presuppositions of what he/she asks for (and how he/she asks for it) as a statement about what they may need (but not ask for) in the present state. For instance, if the person says something that you believe is not true, there may be a problem with how this person makes judgments or decisions.

Process for Specifying Ecology, Planning Intervention:

1. Specify Outcome. A wants outcome. Pick something you've wanted for awhile, but not gotten. B meta-models this outcome, using well-formedness conditions to get:

    *   Desired State

    *   Evidence Procedure

    *   Context

    *   Backtrack

    *   Contrast with Present State. (Use desired state as a filter to know what's relevant).

2. Ecology Tests. B applies all the (9) ecology tests to discover possible harmful consequences. When you find problems with, or objections to, the desired outcome, modify the outcome so that you get only the desired change.

3. Planning Intervention.

    *   When you have a desired outcome that has been thoroughly checked for ecology, think about how you would proceed to make the desired change with the techniques available to you. Chunk down your outcome, using backward planning. Which techniques would you use, in what order, to achieve the outcome?

    *   Take your intervention plan to Trainer or one of the assistants for approval before carrying it out.

    *   Go back and carry out your intervention. (You may want to modify your plan as you proceed).

THE RELEVANCY CHALLENGE

Definition: A verbal and nonverbal communication which requires an individual to link their statement and/or actions with the agreed upon outcome.

Purpose: To keep communication on track, economy of movement

Uses:

1. separates need-to-know and need-not-to-know information

2. serves as a break state

3. prevents irrelevant, interfering behavior

EXAMPLES:

Would you please connect that question with the outcome we're presently working on?

I don't understand the relevance of that remark with respect to what we're doing here right now. Please explain.

Your last statement throws me. How is that pertinent to what this part of the meeting is about?

INFORMATION GATHERING FRAMES HOMEPLAY

In the following statements, the effective communicator is in the process of gathering information. Given this information, which of the information-gathering frames is used in each example? Circle the correct response.

1.   Your client wants to be able to hold, touch and be more affectionate with his wife. He then begins to talk about his boss and that he would like to smash his boss's face. You ask: "How would smashing your boss get you closer to your wife?"

   a) Relevancy Challenge   b) "As If" Frame   c) Ecology Frame

2.   You are seeing this client for the first time. She talks of how she argues with her husband, hates her job, and basically that life is a drag. She goes on and on and finally you say, "Yes, I can feel that you are being dragged down and I'm wondering what you want for yourself?"

   a) Ecology Frame   b) Outcome Frame   c) "As If" Frame

3.   You are seeing a client who claims he has a phobia. He talks of not being able to leave a certain area of the city he lives in. You have him imagine driving his car outside that area (he's in the picture). As he does this, you notice minimal responses, and he says that "nothing much happened." You ask him, "How would your life be different and what would you be doing if you were able to leave your area?"

   a) Outcome Frame   b) Ecology Frame   c) Relevancy Challenge

4. You ask an employee to look into the past and describe how she looked, sounded and felt while working in a job position she really enjoyed. You then have her go into the future and describe how she will look, feel and respond to people when she is getting the responses from colleagues that she wants. You then ask her to create an image of the future person, step into that picture, and become the future person.

    a) "As If" Frame   b) Outcome Frame   c) Ecology Frame

5. A woman comes in to you complaining of disappointment in relationships. When you ask her how, specifically, relationships have been disappointing she accesses lower left, uper left, down right, sighs and says, "I'm not sure. I just want a relationship that has fulfillment." When you ask her how she would know if a relationship was fulfilling, she accesses lower left, upper left, down right and says, "I'm not sure." She pauses and accesses upper right, down right and says, "But, I'd know when I had one." You ask her, "Are you sure?" She accesses lower left, upper left, down right, sighs and says, "I guess not."

    What do you know about the structure of her experience given the information that you have gathered so far?

GO INSIDE, DEVELOP A STATE OF MIND

Purpose: Going inside simply means to retrieve a memory and, in so doing, retrieve a state.

1. Determine your outcome. Why are you going inside? You will want to know what you're after so you will know when it's OK to come back out. Example: I'd like to recall a pleasant experience.

2. With your outcome in place, turn your awareness to your inner processes. You may begin a dialogue with yourself. You may begin to see pictures or you may begin to get feelings. Either way, start by turning your attention inward.

3. Once you get something, intensify it. Make it brighter, louder or feel it more intensely. As you identify the information content, develop the state more fully by bringing in the other systems. You might use sounds that go with the state to help you see the pictures. You might use the feelings you get to bring up an old memory of a picture that went with those feelings in the past.

4. Continue to branch into each of the systems until a full visual, auditory and kinesthetic representation is achieved (a fully represented state).

INTRODUCTION TO REFRAMING

A very old Chinese Taoist story describes a farmer in a poor country village. He was considered very well-to-do, because he owned a horse which he used for plowing and for transportation. One day his horse ran away. All his neighbors exclaimed how terrible this was, but the farmer simply said, "Maybe."

A few days later the horse returned and brought two wild horses with it. The neighbors all rejoiced at his good fortune, but the farmer just said, "Maybe."

The next day the farmer's son tried to ride one of the wild horses; the horse threw him and broke his leg. The neighbors all offered their sympathy for his misfortune, but the farmer again said, "Maybe."

The next week conscription officers came to the village to take young men for the army. They rejected the farmer's son because of his broken leg. When the neighbors told him how lucky he was, the farmer replied, "Maybe."

The meaning that any event has depends upon the "frame" in which we perceive it. When we change the frame, we change the meaning. Having two wild horses is a good thing until it is seen in the context of the son's broken leg. The broken leg seems to be bad in the context of peaceful village life; but in the context of conscription and war, it suddenly becomes good.

This is called **reframing**: changing the frame in which a person perceives events in order to change the meaning. When the meaning changes, the person's responses and behaviors also change.

Reframing is not new. Many fables and fairy tales include behaviors or events that change their meaning when the frames around them change. The different-looking chick seems to be an ugly duckling, but he turns out to be a swan - more beautiful than the ducks he has been comparing himself to. Reindeer Rudolf's funny-looking red nose becomes useful for guiding Santa's sleigh on a foggy night.

Reframing is also the pivotal element in the creative process: it is the ability to put a commonplace event in a new frame that is useful or enjoyable. A friend of physicist Donald Glaser pointed to a glass of beer and jokingly said "Why don't you use *that* to catch your subatomic particles?" Glaser looked at the bubbles forming in the beer, and went back to his lab to invent the "bubble chamber," similar to the Wilson cloud chamber, for detecting the paths of particles in high energy physics experiments. Arthur Koestler, in The Art of Creation, calls this process "bisociation:" the ability to simultaneously associate an event in two very separate and different contexts.

In general communication theory there is a basic axiom that a signal only has meaning in terms of the frame or context in which it appears. The sound of a squeaky shoe on a busy sidewalk has little meaning; the same sound outside your window when you are alone in bed means something else altogether. A light in a church belfry is simply that. But to Paul Revere it meant that the British were coming, and also how they were coming: "One if by land, and two if by sea." The light only has meaning in terms of the previous instructions that established a frame - an internal context that creates meaning.

Reframing appears widely in the therapeutic context. When a therapist tries to get a client to "think about things differently" or "see a new point of view" or to "take other factors into consideration," these are attempts to reframe events in order to get the client to respond differently to them.

Explicit conceptualizations of reframing have been used by a number of therapists who understand that "problem behavior" only makes sense when it is viewed in the context in which it occurs. These include a number of therapists with a family or systems orientation, notably Paul Watzlawick and the Mental Research Institute group in Palo Alto, and Jay Haley and Salvador Minuchin and the group at the Philadelphia Child Guidance Clinic. These therapists generally use what is called "content reframing." They have designed specific reframing interventions such as "prescribing the symptom" and "paradoxical injunction" which effectively reframe behavior in order to change it. They also use techniques of directly intervening to change the actual external physical context in which the behavior occurs.

Virginia Satir used a great deal of reframing in her work, from simple redefinitions to more elaborate reframing via psychodrama in her "parts parties" and "family reconstructions."

Carl Whitaker reframes with nearly everything he says to the families that he works with. Symptoms become reframed as accomplishments or skills, "sanity" becomes craziness, and "craziness" becomes sanity.

A more elaborate and "all-purpose" method of reframing, called **"six-step" reframing**, was developed by Bandler and Grinder. It's an excellent all-purpose model that will work for a great many things. It's got future-pacing and an ecological check built into it, so you can hardly go wrong if you follow the procedure congruently and with sensory experience.

However, that's only one model of reframing. There are several other models. One of them, called **"content reframing,"** is the most common way that reframing is done in therapy. We call it content reframing because, unlike six-step reframing, you need to know specific content in order to make the reframe. There are two kinds of content reframing, and I'm going to give you an example of each. One of my favorite examples is this: one day in a workshop, Leslie Cameron-Bandler was working with a woman who had a compulsive behavior - she was a clean-freak. She was a person who even dusted light bulbs! The rest of her family could function pretty well with everything the mother did except for her attempts to care for the carpet. She spent a lot of her time trying to get people not to walk on it, because they left footprints - not mud and dirt, just dents in the pile of the rug.

When this particular woman looked down at the carpet and saw a footprint in it, her response was an intense negative kinesthetic gut reaction. She would rush off to get the vacuum cleaner and vacuum the carpet immediately. She was a professional housewife. She actually vacuumed the carpet three to seven times a day. She spent a tremendous amount of time trying to get people to come in the back door, and nagging at them if they didn't, or getting them to take their shoes off and walk lightly. Have you ever tried to walk without any weight on your feet? The only person I've seen do it is the guy at the beginning of that old TV program, *Kung Fu*, where they roll out the rice paper, and he walks down it without leaving footprints. When you can do that, you can marry this woman and live in her house.

This family, by the way, didn't have any juvenile delinquents or overt drug addicts. There were three children, all of whom were there rooting for Leslie. The family seemed to get along fine if they were not at home. If they went out to dinner, they had no problems. If they went on vacation, there were no problems. But at home everybody referred to the mother as being a nag, because she nagged them about this, and nagged them about that. Her nagging centered mainly around the carpet.

What Leslie did with this woman is this: she said, "I want you to close your eyes and see your carpet, and see that there is not a single footprint on it anywhere. It's clean and fluffy - not a mark anywhere." This woman closed her eyes, and she was in seventh heaven, just smiling away. Then Leslie said *"And realize fully that that means you are totally alone, and that the people you care for and love are nowhere around".* The woman's expression shifted radically, and she felt terrible! Then Leslie said "Now, put a few footprints there and look at those footprints and know that the people you care most about in the world are nearby." And then, of course, she felt good again.

You can call that intervention "trade feelings" if you like. You can call it a change of strategy. You can call it anchoring. You can call it lots of things, but one useful way to think about it is as reframing. In this particular kind of reframing <u>the stimulus in the world doesn't actually change, but its *meaning* changes</u>. You can use this kind of reframing any time you decide that the stimulus for a problem behavior doesn't really need to change - that there's nothing inherently bad about it.

The other choice, of course, would have been to attack the rest of the family and get them all to shape up and not leave footprints. This woman's mother tried that; it didn't work very well.

If people have a sensory experience that they don't like, what they don't like is their *response* to it. One way of changing the response is to understand that the response itself is not based on what's going on in sensory experience. If you change what the experience *means* to them, their response will change.

What we know about the woman who kept everything clean is that she engages some strategy that allows her to decide when it's time to feel bad. She doesn't feel bad on vacations, or in a restaurant. My guess is that when she walks into somebody else's house and it's messy, she doesn't feel bad, because her response has to do with ownership. Her home is her territory; she only feels bad within certain limits. She may not consider the garage or the backyard to be in her territory. Some people keep their houses spotless, but they don't consider their children's rooms to be part of the house, so they don't feel bad about them when they're dirty.

These are all people, of course, who use negative motivation strategies. As they walk into the kitchen and see dirty dishes everywhere, they go "Ugh!" In order to make the bad feeling go away, they have to wash all the dishes. Then they can stand back and go "Ahhh!" When they walk into a clean hotel room, they don't go "Ahhh!" because it's not theirs. So there's some kind of a decision strategy at work.

One way to help this family would be to alter this woman's strategy. Her strategy has some other characteristics which are unpleasant for her. But to solve the immediate problem and achieve a very limited therapeutic gain, all you need to do is to get her to have a positive feeling about one thing: the carpet. That is not a pervasive change, but it's something you should be able to do. This is *especially* true for those of you engaged in the business world, because content reframing is the essence of sales.

Some people call this "redefining" or "relabeling." Whatever you call it, what you are doing is attaching a new response to some sensory experience. You leave the content the same and put another piece of meaning around it - the same *kind* of meaning that the person has already made. The clean-freak mother makes a judgment that when she sees this sensory experience, it means something important enough to feel bad about. If you can define the footprints as being something important enough to feel good about, then her response will change.

To get a change, it's very essential that you have congruent supportive nonverbal analogues as you deliver the reframe. You have to do it with a serious facial expression and tone of voice.

Virginia Satir was a master at content reframing. One of Virginia's main maneuvers to anchor new responses in the family was to do content reframing. Let me give you an example of one I saw her do. I almost blew it for her, because I cracked up when she did it. That's not appropriate in a family therapy situation, so I began coughing. That's always a good cover: when you laugh, you can go into coughing right away, and no one will notice.

Virginia was working with a family. The father was a banker who was professionally stuffy. He must have had a degree in it. He wasn't a bad guy; he was very well-intentioned. He took good care of his family, and he was concerned enough to go to therapy. But basically he was a stuffy guy. The wife was an extreme placator, in Virginia's terminology. For those of you who are not familiar with that, a placator is a person who will agree with anything and apologize for everything. When you say, "It's a beautiful day!," the placator says, "Yes, I'm sorry!"

The daughter was an interesting combination of the parents. She thought her father was the bad person and her mother was the groovy person, so she always sided with her mother. However, she acted like her father.

The father's repeated complaint in the session was that the mother hadn't done a very good job of raising the daughter, because the daughter was so stubborn. At one time when he made this complaint, Virginia interrupted what was going on. She turned around and looked at the father and said "You're a man who has gotten ahead in your life. Is this true?"

"Yes."

"Was all that you have just given to you? Did your father own the bank and just say, 'Here, you're president of the bank'?"

"No, no. I worked my way up."

"So you have some tenacity, don't you?"

"Yes."

"Well, there is a part of you that has allowed you to be able to get where you are, and to be a good banker. And sometimes you have to refuse people things that you would like to be able to give them, because you know if you did, something bad would happen later on."

"Yes."

"Well, there's a part of you that's been stubborn enough to really protect yourself in very important ways."

"Well, yes. But, you know, you can't let this kind of thing get out of control."

"Now I want you to turn and look at your daughter, and to realize beyond a doubt that you've taught her how to be stubborn and how to stand up for herself, and that that is something priceless. This gift that you've given to her is something that can't be bought, and its something that may save her life. Imagine how valuable that will be when your daughter goes out on a date with a man who has bad intentions."

Every experience in the world and every behavior is appropriate, given some context, some frame. In the last example, Virginia changed the context. Being stubborn is judged to be bad in the context of banking and in the context of a man trying to take advantage of the daughter on a date. She is really changing the context that the father uses to evaluate the daughter's behavior. Her behavior of being stubborn with him will no longer be seen as her fighting with him. It will be seen as a personal achievement: he has taught her to protect herself from men with bad intentions; and as a result his internal response changes.

A lot of your ability to establish and maintain rapport with your clients is your ability to appreciate that what looks and sounds and feels really weird and inappropriate to you is simply a statement about your failure to appreciate the context within which that behavior is being generated.

Rather than imposing a new context, you can use the client's own resources to find a new context. Your client says, "I want to stop X-ing." You ask, "Is there some place in your life where behavior X is useful and appropriate?" If the client answers, "Yes, there are some places, but in other places X is just a disaster," then you know where that behavior belongs. You just contextualize that behavior, and substitute a new pattern of behavior in the contexts where X was a disaster.

If the client says, "No, it's not appropriate anywhere," you can assist him in finding appropriate contexts by giving him specific representational system instructions. "See yourself performing that behavior and listen to it. . . Now, where did that happen?"

Those are variations on the theme of content reframing. All the reframing models that we use are based on some kind of content reframing. In the stubbornness example we left the meaning of the behavior the same and put it in a new *context*.

Now, what did we alter in the first example I gave of the woman and the footprints?. . .We left the context the same and changed the *meaning* of the behavior in the same context. Everything remained constant except what the behavior *implied*.

FORMATS

ANCHORING - AN INTRODUCTION

An anchor is <u>any stimulus that evokes a consistent response pattern from a person.</u> (Grinder & Bandler, 1981). It can be any stimulus that is received via any of the five senses individually or in combination. Grinder and Bandler define anchoring as the tendency for any one element of an experience to bring back the entire experience. (Lankton, 1979) For example, for many people, the sight, sound, taste, smell, and/or feel of buttered popcorn brings back prior experiences of being in a movie theater. The process by which the buttered popcorn became associated with movie theaters is called "anchoring."

The response may be an external behavior and/or an internal representation. In psychological terms, anchoring undergirds both classical and operant conditioning. In classical conditioning anchoring is the process by which the conditioned stimulus (Pavlov's bell) becomes associated with the unconditioned response (Pavlov's dog salivating). In operant conditioning anchoring is the basis of "shaping" toward desired behaviors/states or away from undesired ones. In operant learning, "chaining" and "back-chaining" both involve a series of anchors.

The field of NLP has moved the science of learning one step further in that the **well-formedness conditions** that must be present for anchoring to occur have been identified. These conditions are as follows:

1. The uniqueness of the anchor

2. The timing of the anchor

3. The intensity of the experience

4. Purity (i.e., there are no other anchors creating competing experiences)

5. That the person be associated in the experience

Although phobias generally are used as examples of anchoring as one-trial learning, many positive anchors also occur the same way. Many of us need only see a circus elephant to instantly recall the feelings, sights, sounds, and smells of being "under the Big Top."

Realize that we are anchoring all the time. Every movement, sound, touch, taste, or smell is an anchor. The anchors we create that both solve and create problems are those we deliver at times when the well-formedness conditions for anchoring exist. If you tilt your head in a very specific way at the time that another person is very angry and the well-formedness conditions for anchoring exist, you have set an anchor, a visual anchor specifically. Subsequently, every time you tilt your head in that specific way, the other person will experience anger. If you normally and often tilt your head in that specific way, you may get angry responses from the other person at times when you may not want angry responses. Realize that you are always anchoring: it is impossible not to anchor. The key is to be aware of it and to set anchors that match the internal state and external behavior you desire. And the converse is also true: you are constantly being anchored by your own behaviors, the behaviors of others, and the enviornment around you. (Bretto, 1984)

ANCHORING - OUTLINE

1. Use **calibration skills** to detect when the person is in the experience you want to anchor.

2. Access **desired state** (see Eliciting States handout, page 5 in this section).

3. Make sure person is in the picture (not in a meta position), watch eye movements, and/or ask. Be sure they are **associated**.

4. **Anchor** with a touch, vocal characteristic, gesture, etc. Make sure you can repeat the anchor exactly. One way: As you see person go into experience apply anchor and increase pressure as experience builds, then release as it diminishes.

5. If when you **test** the anchor, you do not see the BMIR (Behavioral Manifested Internal Response) you anticipated then either:

   a) the client was not re-experiencing the actual event; or

   b) you did not anchor the most intense part of the experience; or

   c) you may need to stack the anchor with additional events surrounding the same or similar experience. Remember: a resource state must be at least as powerful as a less-than-resourceful state.

   When a "fired" anchor does not trigger the BMIR you thought you anchored, this is FEEDBACK. Use it accordingly.

Important Aspects of Anchoring:

1. Uniqueness of stimulus (Anchor)

2. Intensity of Response (State Accessed)

3. Purity of Response (State Accessed)

4. Timing of Anchor (Sensory Awareness)

5. Accuracy of duplication of anchor (Behavioral Flexibility)

Anchors can be created in any system: V, A, K, O, G

Methods:

1.	Stacking Anchors:	accessing more than one response of a similar kind (for example, resource states) and anchoring them with only one anchor, thereby increasing the power of the state anchored.
2.	Chaining Anchors:	firing off more than one anchor in succession, thereby creating an automatic bridge between the anchored states (for example, stuck to dissociated to resourceful).
3.	Collapsing Anchors:	firing two or more anchors at the same time, thereby creating an integration between the two anchored states (for example anchors for two parts of a person which have been dissociated from one another).

ELICITING (ACCESSING) AND BUILDING STATES (RESOURCES) GUIDELINES

1. **Personal History**: Time when you/person had this resource - usually more effective to go to different context from the one in which the lack of resource is experienced.

2. **As If**: Someone else who has a particular resource you/person wants. Can be someone known personally, someone (e.g., celebrity, movie star, author, politician, etc.) not known personally but who exists, or is a fictional or historical character.

3. **As If**: Go into the future in order to elicit and create resource state, e.g., "When you finish your degree and have been on your own for several years imagine how you'd feel about yourself when meeting new people."

4. **Constructing**: Start from scratch and structure a resource state. Ve - how/what would you/person be seeing externally? Vi - what, if any, images would you/person be seeing internally? Do the same for each representational system, externally and internally. Literally build the "state" of the desired resource experience.

5. **Chunk Down**: Break resource into several smaller chunks. Elicit experience of each chunk. You can anchor each and chain the sequence together so that you end up with one anchor for the resource, e.g., confidence:

    a. Appreciation of one's ability to recognize needed changes and/or growth.

    b. Ability to learn (ride a bike, etc.).

    c. Knowledge of being able to do something again (ride a bike, make someone smile, etc.).

    d. Excitement.

6. **Stacking**: Anchoring in the same spot or with same V or A stimulus several different examples of the same resource. Can get a couple from the past and stack with a present and/or future experience of resource state.

7. **Behavioral Accessing**: How do you want to feel now? Use your own behavior to elicit resource state in the person in the here and now. Remember pacing and leading and shaping skills. Behavior depends on state of mind, which depends on physiology.

8. **Metaphor**: Tell a story about yourself, a friend, etc., in which person can identify with a resource state in another; e.g., "I'm a very slow learner and that's fine with me because I know once I've learned something I really feel confident about knowing it." You can develop more intricate stories, as long as you remember your outcome is to get the person to identify with a character who has the resource you're helping him/her to develop and build.

9. **Non-Specific Language**: Using Milton Model language patterns (being artfully vague) and calibration to assist person in accessing resources. Go for universal experiences which most people have had; e.g., learning to walk and feeling very good and powerful about that accomplishment; watching a fire or listening to rain on the roof and feeling a sense of comfort and relaxation, etc.

10. **Submodalities**: Changing a critical submodality can often turn an ordinary or negative experience into a potential resource. You can change tone, tempo, volume, emphasis, or content of the words in the A representational system. You can change color, shape, movement, size, location, or content of images in the V representational system. (See Submodality handouts in the Submodality section of manual.) What could you change in the K representational system?

11. **Contrast Frame**: An example of when you/person is not able to do something or feel some way and an example of when you/person can do what he/she/you wants to or feel the way he/she/you wants to. Contrast these two states in order to find the differences. By identifying what's different you are isolating, identifying and accessing the resource(s) that is needed in the situation that is unsatisfactory.

FUTURE PACING

Future Pacing is a technique for helping ensure that new behaviors (skills/resources) will occur when desired by stepping into the future and imagining as fully as possible the experience of using those new behaviors (skills/responses) in the appropriate context. Too often changes that occur in therapy or skills learned in the classroom or changes that occur in a manager's office remain associated (anchored) to the therapist, teacher, manager or the therapist's office, classroom, manager's office, rather than being available to the client in the specific situations where the client most needs the new behavior and/or responses.

The primary method of future pacing new forms of behavior is associating (anchoring) the new behavior or response to sensory stimuli that naturally occur in the applicable context. This method is inherent in the **Six-Step Reframing Format** and the **Change Personal History Format.** Future Pacing can be done very directly. One way is to ask the client, "What is the very first thing you will see, hear, or feel that will indicate you need this resource?" When the specific experience is identified, have the client generate it internally and then associate (anchor) the appropriate resource to it. Then when the stimulus occurs in external experience, it will naturally and unconsciously trigger the appropriate feelings/behavior. The most important function of future pacing is to create a conscious and unconscious connection between a new behavior/response and the situations in which you want it to be used. For instance, associating (anchoring) feelings of passion (the resource) to the feeling of smooth cool sheets, or the sound of his/her name softly whispered, or the sight of a yellow rose, is future pacing the resource of passionate feelings to specific externally occurring experiences. This process can be done with couples by associating (anchoring) the new, more useful responses to phenomena that already occur naturally: how he scratches his head, the sight of their front door, the sound of the television being turned off. Any of these can serve as triggers for initiating some newly acquired behavioral choice on the part of clients. Role playing can also often serve to future pace changes.

But most preferable of all is to present the client with the actual situation in which the new choices need to be expressed. Let's say you have an employee who gets angry and unresourceful every time her immediate supervisor asks her for a progress update on a project. You take time, using the techniques you have learned in your certification training, to create alternative responses internally and/or externally for this employee. The employee feels better and you want to future pace to ensure that she will have the resources available to her with the supervisor. You can take on the behavior of the supervisor which was the original stimulus that led to a less than positive response in your employee and test the response from the employee to you.

What is most important about future pacing is that you don't just assume that the client's conscious mind will automatically take the accomplishments of a session into their everyday lives. Although the conscious mind may try very hard, it usually recalls the new behavior only after it has already failed (by exhibiting the former behavior). Unconscious processes, however, work automatically. It is your task to implant the new choices at the unconscious level, making sure that the triggers for these new, more useful behavioral choices will work and that they are certain of occurring at the appropriate time.

Future pacing is *not* frosting on the intervention cake. Without adequate future pacing, the accomplishments of an intervention are often lost. Future pacing is the final step in any effective communication intervention.

FUTURE PACING FORMAT:

1.   Access and associate (anchor) desired behavior/response.

2.   Decide when/where is the best time to have/do this.

3.   Choose a stimulus in the real world that can be counted on to occur at the chosen time and place (only). This can be an internal or external stimulus.

4.   Represent the stimulus in all systems (VAK) and then also represent the behavior/resource in all systems, either simultaneously or immediately sequentially. This creates a link between the two, so that the stimulus in the real world will "fire off" the internal representation of the desired behavior/resource. By representing both stimulus and resource in all systems, you maximize the probability that the external stimulus will trigger the representation of the behavior even if one or two representational systems are preoccupied with some other content. Representing in only one or two systems is a major reason for failure to remember; therefore, if a desired behavior is not available to you in a context, check if you fully represented it during the future pacing step of your work.

STANDARD SWISH PATTERN

Do in pairs. Instructions are for A to do with B.

1. Determine B's unwanted behavior/response.

2. Have B make a large, bright, <u>associated</u> image of what B sees as or just before the unwanted behavior begins. This picture will include the cues that trigger the unwanted behavior. Calibrate B's external behavior. Have B set this picture aside briefly.

3. Ask B "How would you see yourself differently as a person if you no longer had the unwanted behavior? Make a picture of the you that you would be if you no longer had this difficulty." This picture is not simply a picture of the person not smoking, for instance, but a <u>dissociated</u> picture of themselves being a different kind of person -- more capable, with more choices, or whatever else is important to him/her. Make sure it's a picture that gets a strong positive response. Calibrate external behavior.

4. Have B make a large, bright, associated image of the cues (#2), and put a small, dark picture of the desired state (#3) in the lower right-hand corner.

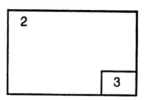

5. "Make the desired state image quickly get bigger and brighter, as the old image becomes dim and overwhelmed. Clear your visual screen, or open your eyes. Repeat this process 5 times." Be sure to have an interruption at the end of each swish, so that the chaining goes only <u>one</u> way. You are creating a <u>direction</u> with this pattern by changing three variables at once: size, brightness, and association/dissociation. Use calibration to confirm internal processes.

6.   Test:

    a.   Make cue image (2). What happens?

    b.   Behavioral test with external cues.

If swish is successful, it will be hard to hold the cue image (2); it will be spontaneously replaced by the desired state image. Likewise, behavioral cues should chain through to the desired state image. Use calibration to confirm report.

CIRCLE OF EXCELLENCE

Purpose: To add resources to a place in your life where you would like more excellence.

1. Identify Excellent State: "What state of excellence would you like to have more present in places in your life? By 'state of excellence' I mean a state in which you have all your resources available to you in a way that allows you to act with full capability."

2. Set up Circle of Excellence: "I'd like you to imagine a circle of excellence on the floor in front of you. What color is yours?" You might even draw this invisible circle on the floor.

3. Access Excellence and Associate it with the Circle: "Think of a time when you were in this state in a way that was fully satisfying to you. When you feel it, step into the circle." As soon as A can observe that B starts to access an excellent state, A motions to B to step forward into the imagined circle on the floor. A and C (director/meta person) make sure that a powerful state is fully accessed, and they both calibrate this state. Be sure you would recognize it when you saw it again. If you don't have sufficient personal history of the state for the exercise, you may simply pretend you do have the history and proceed or you may use any other person's history. You can use a movie hero, a living (or dead) legend or anyone you admire. The amazing thing about your brain is that it can't tell the difference between personal "real" history and personal "imagined" history or the history of others. Also, be sure the person is associated and remember, you can assist them in developing a fully represented state by using predicates to overlap to each representational system.

4. Separator State: "Step back out of the circle." (and distract with a neutral question if necessary to break the state). Your evidence you have broken the state is a physiological shift.

5. Testing: "Now step back into the circle, and find out if it elicits those feelings." A and C make sure that B reaccesses the excellent state fully and automatically (without conscious effort). "Step back out of the circle." (separator state)

6.   Desired Context: "From this point on, anytime I tap you on the shoulder, I want you to step into the circle. Now think of a future situation, or a context, where you would like to have more of this particular excellent state." (Note that this is not an instruction for B to associate into this "problem context." If B does so, A can immediately tap B on the shoulder, so that B steps into the circle of excellence (step 7).

7.   Chaining: "When I touch your shoulder, I want you to immediately step forward into that circle and recover that excellent state." (pause) "How, specifically, might things go wrong in that future situation?," or "What will let you know it's time to have these resources available?" As soon as B begins to access the "problem" state again, A touches B's shoulder, the signal for B to step forward into the circle. A and C observe to be sure that B does quickly access the state of excellence. Suggest B take a moment and note the responses he/she might get from others behaving this way . Are they okay? If not, make any adjustments necessary .

8.   Testing: Ask B to step back out of the circle, (separator state). Then ask B to say a little about the future situation in order to get B to think about it and access it. "Where will that future situation occur?," or "Who else will be there in that future situation," etc. Or, ask "What happens now when you think of what used to go wrong?" Observe to be sure that B only briefly accesses the "problem" state and then automatically accesses the state of excellence. (You can also ask B to report his/her internal experience, but the nonverbal communication is much more important.)

9.   Rotate.

BEHAVIOR GENERATOR STRATEGY

1.   Ask yourself, "If I could already achieve my new goal, what would I look like?"

     (Put your eyes down and to the left)

2.   Picture yourself achieving your goal.

     (Look up and to the right)

3.   To help you visualize:

     A.   Remember a similar successful achievement.

     B.   Model someone else.

     C.   Picture yourself first achieving a smaller part of the goal.

          (Move your eyes up and to the left or the right)

4.   Step into the picture so you feel yourself doing what you saw.

     (Put your eyes and head down and to the right)

5.   Compare the feelings to feelings from a similar past success.

     (Keep your eyes and head turned down and to the right)

6.   If the feelings are not the same, name what you need and add it to your goal. Go back to step 1 and repeat the process with your expanded goal.

     (Move your eyes and head down and to the left)

NEW ORLEANS FLEXIBILITY DRILL #1

Purpose: To develop flexibility of behavior in internal and external states in order to deal with others more resourcefully. There might be people in your life who upset you. It may be appropriate to let them think they are succeeding, when in fact they are not. This exercise teaches the ability to operate on two levels.

1. Person B will describe behavior he finds disturbing in others to A. A will practice behaving in this way in order to elicit a less-than-resourceful state in B. If your group has three participants, person C will act as meta and will assist A in perfecting his role as antagonist to B.

2. A will repeat the behavior several times. The object is to really bother B. The more effective A is at provoking B, the better trained B will become.

3. B goes inside and finds the resources he needs in order to deal with people like A. B anchors these resources within himself. If required, B may stack anchors to develop the resource state more fully. B may also use C to help calibrate and set the anchors.

4. A tests B's resourcefulness by attempting to provoke B. B fires his anchors and either succeeds at thwarting A's provocation or succumbs to it. If B is successful, go on to 5. If less than fully successful, go back to 3 and stack more experiences and/or develop the resource state experiences more fully.

5. B will enter into another interaction with A. B will trigger his anchor prior to the encounter and will be at ease internally but will pretend to have the original non-resourceful response externally as exhibited in 1 above. At the pre-arranged time, B will "snap into" an external state of excellence.

6. If there is a third person involved (C) they monitor the exercise, demand a high quality performance from A (this is a good behavioral flexibility drill) and anchor B if necessary.

7. All participants will ensure members are in appropriate, resourceful states in order to rotate.

NEW ORLEANS FLEXIBILITY DRILL # 2

Purpose: To teach behavioral flexibility. There are behaviors you may find repugnant and can not imagine yourself ever doing. Yet it would be useful to do these behaviors at certain times. This drill teaches the flexibility to perform those behaviors.

1.   In groups of three: A chooses behavior (X) that is uncomfortable for him but would be useful at times. Describe this behavior and the context in which you would like to use it to B.

2.   B will help A find and access the resources he needs to do X.

3.   B provides A's context in order to facilitate A's demonstration of X.

4.   B helps A maintain resourcefulness. A practices his ability to access the resources he needs to X.

5.   Test: During the demonstration with B, A starts out unresourceful and as the scene proceeds the meta observer, C, will signal A to access his resources. Success is achieved when A can access the behavior he wants when he wants it.

6.   All members ensure that fellow participants are in appropriate states to rotate.

7.   NOTE: Both New Orleans Flexibility Drill #1 and #2 can be used to have choices in internal state changes and/or external behavior.

INTERNAL CONFLICT MANAGER FORMAT

Purpose: To assist in conflict resolution when functions of the same person are in conflict.

1.   Identify and clearly separate the functions. Use three identical chairs. Sit in the center chair and place one chair on each side of you. Once the two conflicting parts are identified, place each in a chair. Get a full visual, kinesthetic and auditory representation of each part in each chair. If more parts surface, add more chairs.

2.   Find out what each part wants in order for it to feel fulfilled. Find out why each part is in conflict with the other.

3.   Chunk up to the lowest possible level where both can agree on a shared outcome. If the parts are in serious conflict, you may have to chunk all the way up to the survival of the entity of the person.

4.   Negotiate: What does each part want from the other? What trades must be made? What contracts entered into for each to be satisfied?

5.   Get each part to agree to signal the other when something is needed: e. g., more time, more space, permission, appreciation, attention, affection, etc.

6.   Integrate: Ask each part if it is willing to integrate with the other in order to more efficiently approach the problem and communicate about it. If the answer is yes, integrate the two parts together. If no, keep separate.

7.   Reintegrate: Bring parts back into your body physically.

NEGOTIATING BETWEEN PARTS: OUTLINE

1. Ask the part that is being interrupted (part X) the following questions:

    a.   What is your positive function?

    b.   Which part(s) is (are) interrupting you? (part Y)

2. Ask the same questions of part Y:

    a.   What is your positive function?

    b.   Does X ever interfere with your carrying out your function?

3. If both parts interrupt each other at times, you are now ready to negotiate an agreement. (If not, this model is not appropriate, so switch to another reframing model. If Y interferes with X, but X doesn't interfere with Y, Six-Step Reframing with Y may be most appropriate.)

    a.   Ask Y if its function is important enough that Y would be willing to not interrupt X so that it could receive the same treatment in return.

    b.   Ask X if it was not interrupted by Y, would it be willing to not interrupt Y?

4. Ask each part if it will actually agree to do the above for a specified amount of time. If either part becomes dissatisfied for any reason, it is to signal the person that there is a need to renegotiate.

5. Ecological check: "Are there any other parts involved in this?" "Are there any other parts that interrupt this part, or that utilize these interruptions?" If so, renegotiate.

CREATING A NEW PART: OUTLINE

1. Identify the desired outcome, the function of the part. "I want a part that will achieve X."

2. Access any historical experiences of doing X, or anything similar. Step inside each experience and access all aspects of doing X or parts of X. Go through each memory in all representational systems.

3. Create a detailed set of images of how you would behave if you were actually demonstrating whatever this part of you is going to have you do to achieve the outcome X:

    a. First create a dissociated visual and auditory constructed movie.

    b. When you see a whole sequence that you're satisfied with, step inside the image and go through the whole sequence again from the inside, feeling what it is like to do these behaviors.

    c. If you are not satisfied, go back to 3a and change the movie. Do this until you are satisfied with that fantasy from the inside as well as from the outside.

4. Ecological check. "Does any part object to my having a part which will be in charge of making that fantasy a reality?" Make sure you check all representational systems to find all objecting parts. For each objecting part:

    a. Ask that part to intensify the signal for "yes" and decrease for "no."

    b. Ask "What is your *function* for me?" "What do you do for me?"

    c. If the function doesn't tell you what the part's objection is ask, "What specifically is your objection or concern?"

5.   Satisfy all the objecting parts:

     a.   Redefine the part you are creating to take into account all the functions and concerns of the objecting parts.

     b.   Go back to step 3 and make a new or modified fantasy that will satisfy the concerns of each part that objected.

     c.   Check with every part to make sure that each one is satisfied that this new representation of the new part's behavior will not interfere with function.

6.   Ask your unconscious resources to analyze that fantasy and to pull from it the essential ingredients. Your unconscious is to use this information to build a part and give it *entity*. "Get what you need to know from that fantasy to be able to build a part of you that can do this exquisitely and easily, and at every moment that it needs to be done."

7.   Test the part to make sure it is there:

     a.   Go inside and ask.

     b.   Future pace, repeatedly.

     c.   Behaviorally engage the part to find out if it responds appropriately.

SIX-STEP REFRAMING OUTLINE

1. Identify the pattern (X) to be changed. "I want to stop X'ing but I can't," or "I want to Y, but something stops me."

2. Establish communication with the part responsible for the pattern.

   a. "Will the part of me that makes me X communicate with me in consciousness?" Pay attention to any feelings, images, or sounds that occur in response to asking that question.

   b. Establish the "yes/no" meaning of the signal. Have it increase in brightness, volume, or intensity for "yes," and decrease for "no."

3. Separate the *behavior* pattern X, from the *positive intention* of the part that is responsible for X. The unwanted behavior is only a way to achieve some positive function.

   a. Ask the part that runs X, "Would you be willing to let me know in consciousness what you are trying to do for me by Pattern X?"

   b. If you get a "yes" response, ask the part to go ahead and communicate its intention. If you get a "no" response, proceed with unconscious reframing, presupposing positive intention.

   c. Is that intention acceptable to consciousness? Do you want to have a part of you which fulfills that function?

   d. Ask the part that runs X, "If there were ways to accomplish your positive function that would work as well as, or better than X, would you be interested in trying them out?"

4. Access a creative part, and generate new behaviors to accomplish the positive function.

    a. Access experiences of creativity and anchor them or ask, "Are you aware of a creative part of yourself?"

    b. Have the part that runs X communicate its positive function to the creative part, allow the creative part to generate more choices to accomplish that function, and have the part that used to run X select three choices that are at least as good or better than X. Have it give a "yes" signal each time it selects such an alternative.

5. Ask the part "Are you willing to take responsibility for using the three new alternatives in the appropriate context?" This provides a future pace. In addition you can ask the part at the unconscious level to identify the sensory cues that will trigger the new choices, and to experience fully what it's like to have those sensory cues effortlessly and automatically bring on one of the new choices.

6. Ecological Check. "Is there any part of me that objects to any of the three new alternatives?" If there is a "yes" response, recycle to step 2 above.

(Note: When reframing very dissociated states (such as alcoholism, compulsive overeating, etc.) first, anchor the two states and collapse them: then, proceed with reframing.)

CHANGE PERSONAL HISTORY

1.   Anchor the unwanted or unpleasant feeling.

2.   Use this anchor to assist the client in going back through time to find other times when he/she felt "this" way.

3.   When exaggerations of the expression are noticed, stop the client and have them see the full experience, noting their age when the experience took place. With each exaggerated experience, establish an anchor so you can get back to the specific experience if needed (these anchors can be auditory or kinesthetic).

4.   Once the client has identified three or four such experiences, release that anchor and bring them back to the present.

5.   Ask the client what resource he/she needed to have in those past situations for them to have been satisfying experiences. Be sure the resource is one which influences the client's behavior and subjective experience. Many people think everything would be fine if only the other people were somehow different. The point, however, is for the client to have been different and thus to make new learnings by eliciting different responses from the other people involved in that past experience. Once the needed resource is identified, assist him/her in accessing an experience where he/she genuinely exhibited that resourcefully. Anchor it.

6.   Using the resource anchor have him/her go to each of the already identified past experiences and change history using the added resource. You can use the anchors which designate each of the 3 or 4 experiences to assist them in going directly to them. When he/she is satisfied with the changed experience, have him/her nod and then proceed to the next one. (If your client is not satisfied with the new outcome produced in the old experience move back to step 5. Get another resource or a different resource more appropriate to the specific past experience then proceed on to step 6 again or collapse positive and negative anchors simultaneously, holding positive anchor slightly longer before releasing.)

7.   Have him/her remember the past experience with no anchors to discover if indeed those memories have subjectively changed.

8.   When past experiences have been changed, have him/her future pace. That is, to imagine the next time a situation similar to the past ones is likely to occur, suggesting he/she take the needed resource along. Use no anchors. This is a way of testing whether the changes have generalized.

V/K DISASSOCIATION - FAST PHOBIA CURE

The steps for utilizing three-place visual-kinesthetic disassociation are:

1. Establish a powerful anchor for solid comfort.

2. Holding the anchor, have the client visualize himself/herself out in front in the very first scene of the traumatic incident, making it a "still-shot". So he/she is sitting there, next to you, seeing his/her younger self before him/her.

3. When he/she can see himself/herself clearly, have him/her float out of his/her body so that he/she can see himself/herself sitting there next to you watching his/her younger self. As such, there are now three of him/her. The visual perspective remains from the third place. Their actual body is in the second and the younger self going through the experience is in the first place. When this three-place disassociation is accomplished, anchor it.

4. Now have the person run the experience through, making sure he/she remains kinesthetically disassociated from the traumatic incident by the use of anchors and by the use of verbal patterns which separate out the three places - *him/her, there; the younger you; that experience; what happened then*, to separate the younger traumatized self from - *you, here, today, watching yourself*, etc.

5. When the experience has been completely seen, have the third place float back into second place. (So the visual perspective is being integrated with the actual body position of the client.)

6. Have the present-day person go to the younger one (the one who went through the traumatic experience) and reassure him/her that he/she is from the future, giving the younger self needed comfort and appreciation.

7. When the present-day person can see that the visualized younger self understands, have him/her integrate by bringing that younger part back inside his/her own body.

The following diagram will serve to clarify the steps involved.

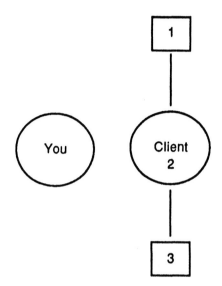

You anchor the client (2) to feel secure in the here and now. Then the client visualizes his/her younger self (1), then floats out of his/her body to the visual perspective of (3). Anchor this disassociative state. From (3) the traumatic episode is run through, after which (3) integrates back to (2). Then (2) comforts and reassures (1) and finally (2) brings (1) back into (2) and only you and your client are there.

If at any time your client should collapse realities and begin re-experiencing the feelings contained within the past trauma, stop. Bring them back to the here and now completely, reestablish the first powerful positive anchor and begin again. In a few cases I have had to stop and start this process two or three times before the person was able to remain adequately disassociated such that the whole process could be completed.

This format is careful to disassociate when useful and then to fully integrate the disassociated parts of the person. This is a most effective method for dealing with those cases that involve a very powerful past experience that negatively influences a client's present experience. Clients describe this process as, "Bringing things into perspective," "I can remember it, but I'm not overwhelmed by it anymore," "I thought I just wanted to forget that awful thing ever happened, but now I think it's good," or "I learned a lot from it."

NEGOTIATIONS

ARBITRATION AND NEGOTIATION

The process of arbitration and negotiation provide a good example of the application of NLP principles to the handling of interference in organizations. The steps of the procedure are a slight modification of the reframing TOTE.

1. Establish the specific outcome of each individual involved in the conflict in relation to a meta-outcome that all parties agree upon.
    For example, have each person make the following statement, filling in the blanks. "I specifically want the outcome of _____, for the purpose of _____."

    Their purpose will be a meta-outcome. If their meta-outcomes do not at this point match one another in some way, have each of them repeat the process again, this time substituting the meta-outcome each has come up with in the last statement as the specific outcome of this statement. Keep repeating this process with the newly generated meta-outcomes until you arrive at a general goal that everyone agrees upon. Then anchor their agreement.

    Establishing that all of the parties actually have the same goal immediately puts a frame around the rest of the interaction. When all parties agree that they are attempting to achieve the same outcome, their conflicts become reframed as a matter of detail to be worked out, and the rest of your task is essentially team-building.

    It also helps to establish from the very beginning that the *conflict* between the negotiating parties is counter-productive to achievement of their meta-outcomes and specific outcomes, and to have all parties agree that it should be resolved as quickly as possible.

2. Get all parties to agree again on what a successful outcome of the negotiation would be. For instance, find out what would constitute an acceptable decision. And if a successful settlement is not made, find out what further information is needed, who will get it, and how the information will be gathered.

3. As the parties are considering the issues and making decisions about what is to be an appropriate outcome to the negotiation, observe their strategies for decision making.

4. Access reference structures for possible resources, such as, "Have you ever been able to settle a negotiation before in a way that you were satisfied with?" or "Has there ever been a time when you were able to communicate with someone really effectively and surprised yourself by setting something right that you had previously thought would never get straightened out?" Covertly anchor these experiences so that you can put them into play at the appropriate time.

5. Control the analogue communications of the parties so that they produce no adverse effects on the negotiation proceedings. We believe that most of what actually gets communicated in our verbal interactions is the result of the accompanying nonverbal or analogue cues. When we arbitrate for organizations (or work with groups, as in family therapy) we pay attention to the control and nonverbal portions of the interactions more than we do the verbal portions. In our experience, this has made a tremendous difference in the parties' responses to one another. If an individual, for example, were to raise his voice and point his finger at someone while making a point or statement, and if we noticed that the person to whom he directed his nonverbal gestures began to tense up and stop breathing (indicating a negative response), we would have the person who made the statement stop, change their analogue and repeat the exact same statement. In practically every instance this will change the other individual's response to, or understanding of, the statement.

6. Utilize the decision-making and motivation strategies of each party to influence their decision-making processes (especially if you are a negotiator) when you think it is appropriate or necessary, making use of any anchors that you have established.

7. Act as a translator (especially if you are an arbitrator) reinterpreting and recording what has been said into the vocabulary of the different representational systems when you find that differences in the strategy of the individual parties are getting in the way. Establishing some rapport with each party via overt or covert pacing will also be a very effective tool.

8.   As you carry out the negotiation process, start with the meta-outcome that everyone is in agreement with and move on to specifics from there, gathering information and altering each party's position until you can find the middle ground. Any time that you run into problematic disagreements return to the meta-outcome to reestablish the positive framework.

NEGOTIATIONS

One way of thinking about the sequence of behaviors during a negotiation is as follows:

SEQUENCE CONTENT	NLP PATTERNS TO APPLY

Before the meeting:

1. Personal Resources:

Ensure state appropriate to task at hand.

Awareness of physiology
Self anchoring

2. Outcome:

Figure out well formed outcome for that paticular negotiation. Plan also maximum goal and minimum acceptable result beforehand (do not negotiate with yourself during the meeting).

Outcome frames
Well-formedness conditions

In the meeting:

1. Personal Resources:

Ensure state appropriate to task at hand.

Awareness of physiology
Self anchoring

2. Rapport:

Establish contact and sufficient rapport to elicit the responses you need.

Behavioral flexibility
Body, voice, predicate pacing

3.   **Frame:**

Set frames for the meeting that will provide sufficient leverage for some forward movement. The frame of the negotiation itself should provide leverage to maintain behaviors within acceptable bounds and ensure that all parties share some positive (albeit temporary) goal.

Frames
Anchors (for the agreement to the frame)
Relevancy Challenge (use throughout to defend frames)

4.   **Statement of Positions:**

When each side makes a summary statement of position and desired outcome for the negotiation. This provides the content basis for the negotiation.

Predicates
Accesing cues
Language model

5.   **Chunking Up and Down:**

This is where definition of positions is refined and intent behind positions discovered. It provides the movement possibility even with rigid starting points. Each time a chunk up provides a bridge of agreement, anchor that agreement.

Intent Frame/Chunking Up
Language model
Anchoring

6.   **Backtrack:**

Cover all agreements made (use anchors to remind and reinforce) and calibrate for any mis-understandings. Use "As-If" frame to test for solidity of agreements made (devil's advocate position).

Backtrack
Calibration
Anchoring

7. Future Pace:

Run through parties' commitments
to next step, providing contextual
markers which you know will occur
in their environment and which may
serve as reminders to carry out the
steps agreed to.

Future pace

8. Closing Ritual:

Shake hands or other appropriate
gesture serving as behavioral marker
confirming agreements made and
closing the negotiation.

THE NEGOTIATOR'S CHECK LIST

Pre-Negotiation Checks:

Outcomes:

What specifically are the outcomes for this negotiation? Are there covert outcomes as well? (e.g., determining compatibility of client for long term relationship).

Evidence Procedure:

How will you know that the negotiation has been completed? What evidence will you see, hear or touch that will confirm to you that you have finished? What will you do next with the information generated? (E.g., "As If" forward in time - to whom will you present it, what will they be asking for?)

Maximum/Minimum:

Never negotiate with yourself while negotiating with the client. Know in advance what the terms you want are and what the minimum you can agree to, plus any provisions covering this minimum.

Support Materials:

Documentary or other evidence supporting your position which can be shown to the client during the negotiation.

Setting:

Flexible seating arrangements to provide for physical confrontation or alignment choices. Arrange signal system with colleague to provide a 'time out' for you if you need it.

During the Negotiation:

Opening Frames:

Statement of outcomes in broad terms to gain agreement from all parties about the overall intentions for the negotiation. This is especially important in mediation situations since it sets up the leverage position for the mediator which can be used to challenge for irrelevant behaviors (e.g., later in the mediation one party starts shouting at the other and mediator challenges, "Hold on a moment, we agreed at the beginning that we were meeting to try to find some resolution of this situation. Please tell me how shouting at Fred is going to help that?").

Evidence Procedure:

To ensure that all parties have translated their outcomes (which will probably be stated at a fairly high level of abstraction) into real world events which would occur and hence consider consequences.

Establishment of Positions:

Statement by all parties of their positions and needs. (Negotiator will probably prefer to ask only other parties' position and keep their own hand to themselves for as long as possible, but in mediation it's useful to hear a full statement by all sides, watching carefully the other person's non-verbal responses so that you know what their key objections will be.)

Chunking of Information:

Chunking down wards from the statement of positions to ensure a sufficient degree of specificity that negotiation points are well defined in real world terms (e.g., not 'more money', but how much more, not 'losses', but which losses specifically, etc.) so that discussions occur at the same logical level.

Chunking up wards to find intents and possible bridges across points of difference (e.g., "A" must have the contract signed by Wednesday; "B" cannot sign till Friday: what makes necessary and what prevents - by finding the intention behind the statements it may well be possible to find a solution.)

Maxima/Minima List:

Use deviations from Maxima list as conditional close (e.g., "So if I could persuade my directors to reduce the rate of interest from 15% to 14% we would have a contract?").

Stuck Situations:

Where movement forward stops check the following:

Do you have rapport? Check body and voice mirroring.

Are you talking the same language? Check for visual, auditory or kinesthetic words.

Are you talking about the same things? Check specificity of language and use the precision language model as necessary to confirm.

Can we jump this situation by finding a new frame of reference? Remember the farmer who lost his horse?

Can we leave this point for further consideration by all parties and close on all other points? Further information may be developed which will shed new light or even render the point in question meaningless.

If all else fails, change anything! Behavioral flexibility to distract, gain attention, surprise, amuse, challenge, frighten, reassure. Physiology is also the leverage point for your client's internal state - maybe get them to go for a cup of coffee with you. Physiological movement may trigger movement of internal state.

Backtrack:

At the close, cover the main points agreed to with special attention to action items to ensure that what you thought they agreed to was what they thought they agreed to and that what you thought they would do afterwards was what they thought they would do also!

Later:

Like the golf pro, review in your mind the transaction and note anything you would have done differently. Try to come up with several choices and think them through as preparation for future negotiations.

SELF-PACED EXERCISE

FOR NEGOTIATIONS AND RESOLVING DISAGREEMENTS

---

1. Write a RESPONSE to each of the sentences below (as if someone had made the statement to you, and you were replying to their statement) -- a response which matches the Representational System expressed.

2. Construct two sentences, each of which TRANSLATES your response into another Representational System (as if you were restating the exact same idea to a third person whose Representational System you know to be different).

1. STATEMENT: It looks as if we can quickly pull out of this prolonged slump.

   RESPONSE (MATCH): _____

   RESTATEMENT (TRANSLATE): _____

   _____

2. STATEMENT: I want to get my intuitions honed to an even finer edge.

   RESPONSE (MATCH): _____

   RESTATEMENT (TRANSLATE): _____

   _____

3.   STATEMENT: This is a most distasteful chore; it has soured me on the
                   entire project.

           RESPONSE (MATCH):   _____

           RESTATEMENT (TRANSLATE):   _____

           _____

4.   STATEMENT: Things surely seem to be falling into place the way they
                   should.

           RESPONSE (MATCH):   _____

           RESTATEMENT (TRANSLATE):   _____

           _____

5.   STATEMENT: As the prospects for change get brighter, everything else
                   will click automatically.

           RESPONSE (MATCH):   _____

           RESTATEMENT (TRANSLATE):   _____

           _____

6.   STATEMENT: I love it when I get a lot of static for trying something new.

           RESPONSE (MATCH):   _____

           RESTATEMENT (TRANSLATE):   _____

           _____

7.   STATEMENT: She keeps her enthusiasm under tight reins.

           RESPONSE (MATCH):   _____

           RESTATEMENT (TRANSLATE):   _____

           _____

8. STATEMENT: If you can remain quiet for just a few seconds a day, the richness of the world will become more pronounced.

    RESPONSE (MATCH): _____

    RESTATEMENT (TRANSLATE): _____

_____

MEETINGS

SUCCESSFUL MEETINGS

Business meetings are an invaluable communication tool. When used effectively, they can produce decisions that all participants actively support. But although essential to the successful operation of a business, meetings can be the most costly communication activity in an organization. Take a minute and consider the salaries of the individuals in a meeting and think about what it is costing per hour. Also, let's take a minute and generalize the concept of meetings. Meetings can be defined as a coming together or an assembly. Whether our profession is technically in the business arena or not we are engaged regularly in assemblies with others hoping to achieve some desired result.

Lack of preparation is often a major reason managers feel that time spent in meetings is unproductive. In addition, most managers have never received training on how to conduct a meeting, and few companies provide guidelines. To ensure success, carefully consider when to hold a meeting and know what is to be accomplished. A rule of thumb is that if information can be conveyed in writing, over the telephone, or a one-on-one visit, do not hold a meeting. Reserve meeting time for aiding decision making and developing relationships.

When planning a meeting be sure to have specific objectives and limit participation to those who have the authority to make and carry out decisions, have knowledge that they are willing to contribute, and be able to provide, or need to receive, information.

In this section you will find a specific model for conducting effective meetings which was developed by John Grinder. Please reference earlier sections of the manual for specifics on the communication tools referenced. Also, the section on procedures from John Grinder and Mike McMaster's book Precision provides additional information.

THE MEETING FORMAT

I. Pre Meeting

1. Determine the Outcome: What do you want as a result?

2. Develop an Evidence Procedure: How will you know if you have it?

3. Develop Options: What will happen if. . . . .?

4. Establish membership and agenda. Remember the 2/3rds Rule

II. Opening

1. Establish Rapport and Access Resourceful States.

2. State Outcome and Evidence Procedure.

3. Get consensus on (2).

III. Discussion

1. Relevancy Challenge

2. As If Frame

3. Counter Example

4. Chunking

5. Backtrack Frame

6. Meta Model

7. Procedures - Difference, Missing Link, Recycling

IV. Closing

1. Summarize Outcome(s) - Backtrack Frame

2. State next step(s)

PROCEDURES

Procedures were developed by John Grinder and Michael McMaster (1981) and designed for specific uses at specific stages of information processing.

I.   Difference Procedure:

The Difference Procedure is appropriate at any point in the process of eliciting high quality information where the communicator has identified both (a portion of) the Present State and (a portion of) some Desired State or desirable situation which has a positive characteristic which could be used as part of the Desired State. The question itself simply requests information about other characteristics of the Desired State or desirable situation which may help to explain the presence of the positive characteristic in the Desired State and its absence in the Present State.

There is no immediate language cue to inform the information processor that the question is to be asked as there is in the Meta Model questions. The cue or test for appropriateness for the Difference Question is whenever both a Present State and some Desired State (one which has some positive characteristic that would be desirable to incorporate into the Desired State) have been identified. There are, however, a number of language cues which signal that this appropriateness test for the Difference Question is satisfied. Specifically, these are:

1.   Immediately following the challenge of a Nominalization.

2.   Immediately following the challenge of a Comparative.

3.   Immediately following a statement using the word(s) *except, with the exception of, different, difference, not the same as, not counting.*

II.   Missing Link Procedure:

The Missing Link is a refinement of the relevancy challenge. In the Relevancy Challenge we asked for further specification because the relation to the Desired Outcome was not apparent. Here we are asking for further specification, not because we don't understand the connection but because there might be a relatively less specified action which would indicate a new direction for alternatives. Let's say that a sales manager and his general manager had agreed "to create a new reporting method which would increase the control over sales." The first suggestion might have been to keep logs of sales call activity. A visual representation of this stage might look like the following:

Increase control over sales

Create new reporting system

Keep logs of sales call activity

Now, if the Missing Link question, "What will keeping logs do to attain the desired outcome?" were asked, the response might generate the less specified verb phrase, "Use information not contained in the accounting system." That is, the purpose of keeping and using sales logs for reporting is that the sales manager is using that information to judge his salesmen and their efforts and he would like to be judged on the same basis. A more general statement of this possibility has now been added.

Increase control over sales

Create new reporting system

Use non-accounting data in the reporting system (new)

Keep logs of sales call activity

This new representation provides the opportunity to direct the search for alternatives into the area of common performance criteria and will lead to the likelihood of discovering a better solution using orders taken.

III.   Recycle Procedure:

The Recycle Procedure is appropriate whenever a word or phrase is so rich with potential hidden material that it might be profitable to return to it. This procedure can be used when:

1.   An action (verb) phrase is being pursued to develop a number of alternative courses of action or alternatives, or,

2.   A sentence or phrase has a number of words or parts each of which can be profitably developed.

The Recycle Procedure is like a memo to return to a particular point. It ensures that the information processor won't get lost in following a particular track and fail to return to a place which he selected as potentially profitable. In our experience, many information processors fail to return after one track leads to a dead end and lose opportunities to solve problems effectively. We have found that making a visual representation or note can be the most effective way to learn this procedure and that many experienced communicators continue to use the technique of making these notes.   .

A whole tree structure can be developed and will help to keep everyone involved aware of alternatives and where they are in the procedure. A simple procedure of writing down the action which is being specified as a reminder of the return point may be sufficient: For more complex problems, a list of verb phrases can be made and each item circled as it is being developed and checked when complete.   Any of these procedures can be effective when the purpose is to generate a maximum number of alternative actions such as in the Brainstorming phase of discussion.

Each action should be returned to until all possible alternatives have been generated. A variation of the Unspecified Verb Challenge will be appropriate here. After the first challenge to an Unspecified Verb, the Recycle Procedure will be accomplished by the question, "How else might we . . .(verb)?" The word "else" will be repeated until no more alternatives are offered.

The Recycle Procedure is also appropriate when applied to an initial verbal representation. The initial statement is a highly coded representation of a complete map or representation. For instance, the statement, "We need to get rid of slow moving inventory" has a number of elements which all need to be expanded to be of high enough quality for an action plan.

Each of the following questions *for this particular example*, needs to be answered before any precise understanding of what has been proposed can be assumed:

1.   Who, specifically, needs to take the action(s)?

2.   What inventory, specifically, is being considered as "slow moving?"

3.   How, specifically, is it to be "got rid of?"

All of these individual parts need to be considered to arrive at an adequately precise understanding before action is taken. Missing any one of them will leave a gap which could result in unwarranted action or the inability to obtain feedback or maintain accountability. A full specification will provide full control.

COPYRIGHT ACKNOWLEDGMENTS

COPYRIGHT ACKNOWLEDGMENTS

BIBLIOGRAPHY

NEURO-LINGUISTIC PROGRAMMING

BIBLIOGRAPHY

Ager, S. "Manipulation: It's the Latest Brain Game: How to Get the Response You're Seeking." San Jose Mercury and News. (January 8, 1980) Pp. D1-D2.

Allen, Keith Loren. "Investigation of the Effectiveness of Neurolinguistic Programming Procedures in Treating Snake Phobias." (Doctoral dissertation. University of Missouri at Kansas City, 1982.) Dissertation Abstracts International. (1982) 43(3): 861B.

Anon. "Behavior." Time Magazine. (December 19, 1983): 79.

_____. "Bodies Change With Personality." Imagery Article, Brain Mind Bulletin. Science American. (December 1984).

_____. "Communicating More Than Meets the Eye." Nation's Business. (1981): 69(2), 72.

_____. "Executive Skills: When They Listen But Do Not Hear." Research Institute of America, Personal Report for the Executive. (December 4, 1979): B.

_____. "Harlan, B. Masten Used Unique Jury Selection Technique." Rapid City Journal. (May 1, 1984).

_____. "NLP." The Boston Globe. (May 4, 1981): 25.

_____. "Tape Leaves Salesman in Stitches." San Francisco Examiner and Chronicle. (April 3, 1983): A5.

_____. "The Learning Curve: Are They Telling You the Truth?" Electrical World. (1980): 94(1), 41.

Andreas, Connirae. "The Relationship of Eye Movements While Information Processing to Sensory Mode." Unpublished doctoral dissertation. University of Colorado, 1983.

_____. "Research review." The VAK. (1982) 1 (3): 1-2

Andreas, Connirae and Steve Andreas. "Neuro-Linguistic Programming: A New Technology for Training." Performance and Instructional Journal. (1982) 21(5): 37-39.

_____. "NLP: A Reply to Steven Schoen." Psychotherapy Newsletter. (1983) 1(2): 19-24.

_____. Change Your Mind and Keep the Change. Moab, UT: Real People Press, 1988.

Anton, J. "Mapping the Mind With Micros." Electronic Education. (October 1982): 11.

Appel, Phillip Robert. "Matching of Representational Systems and Interpersonal Attraction." (Doctoral dissertation, United States, International University, 1983.) Dissertation Abstracts International. (1983) 43(9): 3021B.

Arkatov, J. "Method in the Madness of Acting." Los Angeles Times, Calendar. (July 20, 1986): 43, 54, 55.

Asbell, Henry Calvin. "Effects of Reflection, Probe, and Predicate-Matching on Perceived Counselor Characteristics." (Doctoral dissertation, University of Missouri at Kansas City, 1983.) Dissertation Abstracts International. (1984) 44(11): 3515B.

Atwater, J.M. "Differential Effects of Interventions from the Neuro-Linguistic Programming Meta-Model and General Systems in Early Psychotherapy." Dissertation Abstracts International. (1984) 44: 2887B.

Austin, and G. Laborde. "Study on NLP and Locus of Control." Palo Alto, CA: The VAK.

Bacon, S.C. "NLP and Psychosomatic Illness: A Study of the Effects of Reframing on Headache Pain." Dissertation Abstracts International. (1984) 44(7): 2233B.

Bagley, Dan and Edward Reese. Beyond Selling. Cupertino, CA: Meta Publications, 1987.

Bailey, R. "Neurolinguistic: Information Processing in the Human Biocomputer". J.C. Penney Forum. (November, 1983).

Bandler, Richard. Magic in Action. Cupertino, CA: Meta Publications, 1985.

_____. Using Your Brain - for a CHANGE: Neuro-Linguistic Programming. Connirae and Steve Andreas (eds). Moab, UT: Real People Press, 1985.

Bandler, Richard, and John Grinder. The Structure of Magic - I: A Book About Language and Therapy. Palo Alto, CA: Science and Behavior Books, 1975.

_____. Patterns of the Hypnotic Techniques of Milton H. Erickson, M.D. Vol. 1. Cupertino, CA: Meta Publications, 1975.

_____. Frogs Into Princes. Moab, UT: Real People Press, 1979.

Bandler, Richard, John Grinder and Virginia Satir. Changing with Families. Palo Alto, CA: Science and Behavior Books, 1976.

Barrett, Deidre. "The Hypnotic Dream: Its Relation to Nocturnal Dreams and Waking Fantasies." Journal of Abnormal Psychology, 1979, 88(5): 584-591.

Bateson, Gregory. Communication: The Social Matrix of Psychiatry. New York, NY: W.W. Norton and Company, 1950.

_____. Steps to an Ecology of Mind. New York, NY: Ballantine Books, 1972.

_____. Mind and Nature - A Necessary Unity. New York, NY: Bantam Book, 1972.

Battino, R. "The Humanistic Psychology Movement and the Teaching of Chemistry." Journal of Chemical Education. (1983) 60(3): 224-227.

Baum-Baicker, C., and C deTorres. "Sensory Based Target Strokes." Transactional Analysis Journal. (1982) 12:195-196.

Beale, R. "The Testing of a Model for the Representation of Consciousness." (Doctoral dissertation, The Fielding Institute, 1980.) Dissertation Abstracts International. (1981) 41(9): 3565B.

Beck, C., and E. Beck. "Test of Eye-Movement Hypothesis of NLP: A Rebuttal and Conclusions." Perceptual and Motor Skills, 1984: 58, 175-176.

Bertalanffy, Ludwig von. Robots, Men and Minds. New York, NY: Braziller, 1967.

_____. Problems of Life. New York, NY: Harper and Row, 1951.

Billups, A. "Representational System Congruence (Predicate Matching) as a Dimension of Interpersonal Impact." Dissertation Abstracts International. 44(1): 3517B.

Birholz, Laura S. "Neurolinguistic Programming: Testing Some Basic Assumptions." (Doctoral dissertation, The Fielding Institute, 1981.) Dissertation Abstracts International. (1981) 43(5): 2042B.

Bois, J. Samuel. The Art of Awareness. Wm. C. Brown Co. Publishers, 1966.

Boswell, Louis K., Jr. "The Initial Sensitizing Event of Emotional Disorders." British Journal of Medical Hypnotism, 1961: 12(3).

Bower, Gordon H. "Mood and Memory." American Psychologist. (1981) 36(2): 129-148.

Bradley, E.J. and H. Beidermann. "Bandler and Grinder's Neurolinguistic Programming: Its Historial Context and Contribution". Psychotherapy. 22: 59-62.

Brengle, E.Q. "Preference for Sensory Modality of Mental Imagery and Its Relationship to Stress Reduction Using a Systematic Desensitization Technique." (Doctoral dissertation, Wayne State University, 1979.) Dissertation Abstracts International. (1979) 40(4): 1878B.

Bretto, Charlotte. "Metaphor: The Art of Purposeful Storytelling." Santa Cruz, CA: The Center for Professional Development, 1985.

_____. A Framework for Excellence: A Resource Manual for NLP. Santa Cruz, CA: The Center for Professional Development, 1989.

Bretto, Charlotte, Judith DeLozier, and John Grinder. Leaves Before the Wind. Grinder, DeLozier and Associates, Santa Cruz, CA, 1989.

Brockman, W.P. "Empathy Revisited: The Effect of Representational System Matching on Certain Counseling Process and Outcome Variables." (Doctoral dissertation, The College of William and Mary in Virginia, 1980.) Dissertation Abstracts International. (1981) 41(8): 3421A.

Brockop, D.Y. "What is NLP?" American Journal of Nursing. (July, 1983): 1012-1014.

Brownlee, M. "Communicating Research: NLP - A Highway of Diamonds With (Almost) No One On It?" Journal of Australian Marketing, Advertising and Communication: 3, 42-50.

Buchanan, D.R. and D. Little. "Neurolinguistic Programming and Psychodrama: Theoretical and Clinical Similarities." Journal and Group Psychotherapy, Psychodrama and Sociometry: 36, 144-122.

Burns, F., and L. Nelson. "High Performance Programming: An Operations Model for a New Age." O E Communique: The Professional Organizational Effectiveness/Development Publication of the U.S. Army, 1981: 5(2), 27.

Burton, John K., and Roger H. Brunning. "Interference Effects on the Recall of Pictures, Printed Words, and Spoken Words." Continuing Education Psychology. (1982): 7, 61-69.

Cabot, T. "How to Make a Man Fall in Love With You." Playgirl. (February, 1984): 33-40.

Cameron-Bandler, Leslie. They Lived Happily Ever After: A Book About Achieving Happy Endings in Coupling. Cupertino, CA: Meta Publications, 1978.

_____. Know How. San Rafael, CA: FuturePace, Inc., 1985.

_____. Solutions. San Rafael, CA: FuturePace, Inc., 1985.

Cameron-Bandler, L. D. Gordon, and M. Lebeau. The Emprint Method: A Guide to Reproducing Competence. San Rafael, CA: Future Pace, Inc., 1985.

Carlin, M. "Tuning Your Brain May Help." Rocky Mountain News. (April 24, 1985): 42.

Carpenter, Tom. "Couple Cures Fear, Phobias." City Edition, (Dec. 18-25, 1985) 4(6): 1,6.

Carter, B.D., G. R. Elkins, and S. P. Kraft. "Hemispheric Assymetry as a Model for Hypnotic Phenomena: A Review and Analysis." The American Journal of Clinical Hypnosis. (1982): 24, 204-210.

Casella, P. "Math Strategy and Spelling Strategy for the Apple II." InfoWorld. (June 28, 1982): 52-53.

Cashman, Rita. "The Outcome Frame: Key to Managing for Excellence." Oak Park, IL: Outcome Development Corporation.

Chong, D.K. Auto-hypnotic Pain Control: The Milton Model. New York: Carolton Press, 1979.

Churchill, Teresa. "Making Sense of Thinking," "Seeing Eye to Eye," and "Don't be Thrown for a Loop." Decatur Herald & Review. (August 12, 1984).

Cleveland, B.F., Master Teaching Techniques. Stone Mountain, GA: Connecting Link Press, 1984.

Cody, Steven Gerard. "The Stability and Impact of the Primary Representational System in Neurolinguistic Programming: A Critical Examination." Dissertation Abstracts International. (1983) 44(4): 1232B.

Cole-Hitchcock, S.T. "A Determination of the Extent to Which a Predominant Representational System Can Be Identified Through Written and Verbal Communication and Eye Scanning Patterns." (Doctoral dissertation, Baylor University, 1980.) Dissertation Abstracts International. (1980) 41(5): 1908B.

Colgrass, Michael. "How to Help a Friend (and Yourself)." Jam Magazine. (Oct. 1983): 10-11.

_____. "You Should See Yourself." Jam Magazine. (Dec. 1983): 12.

_____. "Circle of Excellence." Jam Magazine. (Feb. 1984): 38.

_____. "A Matter of Clairaudience." Music Magazine, (May/June, 1986): 38.

Connel, H.S. "NLP Techniques for Salespeople." Training and Development Journal. (Nov., 1984): 44, 46.

Conway, Flor, and Jim Siegelman. "The Awesome Power of the MIND-PROBERS." Science Digest. (1983): 91(9).

Cook, J. "NLP Could Change Your Life." The Reston Times. (June 10, 1982): C1.

Davis, D. I. and L. R. Davis. "Integrating Individual and Marital Therapy Using Neuro-Linguistic Programming." International Journal of Family Psychiatry: 6(1).

Davis, S.L., and D. Davis. "NLP and Marital and Family Therapy." Family Therapy Networker. (May-June 1982): 19.

DeLozier, Judith and John Grinder. Turtles All The Way Down: Prerequisite for Personal Genius. Santa Cruz, CA: Grinder, DeLozier and Associates, 1987.

Dillon, B. "Values and Helping School-Age Children." Canada's Mental Health. (1978): 26, 7.

Dilts, R. "Individual Baseline EEG Patterns and NLP Representational Systems." In R.B. Dilts, J. Grinder, R. Bandler, J. DeLozier, and L. Cameron-Bandler, Neuro-Linguistic Programming Volume 1, Cupertino, CA: Meta Publications, 1980.

_____. "Neuro-Linguistic Programming in Education: Building Blocks for Learning." Behavioral Engineering, Scotts Valley, CA. (1980).

_____. "NLP in Education." Behavioral Engineering. Scotts Valley , CA. (1982).

_____. "Let NLP Work For You." Real Estate Today. (February 1982): 21.

_____. Roots of Neuro-Linguistic Programming: A Reference Guide to the Technology of NLP. Cupertino, CA: Meta Publications, 1983.

_____. Applications of Neuro-Linguistic Programming: A Practical Guide to Communication. Learning. and Change. Cupertino, CA: Meta Publications, 1983.

Dilts, R., and T. D. Green. "Applications of Neuro-Linguistic Programming in Family Therapy." In A.M. Horne and M.M. Ohlsen (eds.) Family Counseling and Therapy. Itasca, IL: F.E. Peacock, 1982.

Dilts, R., J. Grinder, R. Bandler, J. DeLozier, and L. Cameron-Bandler. Neuro-Linguistic Programming I. Cupertino, CA: Meta Publications, 1979.

Dorn, F.F. "The Effects of Counselor-Client Predicate Use Similarity on Counselors Attractiveness." American Mental Health Counselors Association Journal. (January 1983): 22, 30.

_____. "Assessing PRS tem Preference for NLP Using Three Methods." Counselor Education and Supervision. (December 1983): 149-156.

Dorn, F., J. Atwater, R. M. Jereb, and R. Rusell. "Determining the Reliability of NLP Eye-Movement Procedure." The American Mental Health Counselors Association Journal. (1983): 5, 105-110.

Dowd, E.T., and J. Petty. "Effect of Counselor Predicate Matching on Perceived Social Influence and Client Satisfaction." The Journal of Counseling Psychology. (1982): 29, 206-209.

Edwards, S. "Listening to the Body-Talk." McLeans Magazine. (September 13, 1982): 54.

Ehrmantraut, John Edward, Jr. "Comparison of the Therapeutic Relationship of Counseling Students Trained in Neurolinguistic Programming vs. Students Trained on the Carkhuff Model." (Doctoral dissertation, University of Northern Colorado, 1983.) Dissertation Abstracts International. (1984) 4(10): 319B.

Eicher, James. Making the Message Clear: Communicating for Business. Santa Cruz, CA: Grinder, DeLozier and Associates, 1987.

Elgin, Catherine Zincke. "Reference and Meaning: A Tractarian Analysis of Incomensurable Representational Systems." (Doctoral dissertation, Brandies University.) Dissertation Abstracts International. (1975): Philosophy vol. 36/01 - A.

Elgin, Suzette H. The Gentle Art of Verbal Self-Defense. Dorset Press, 1980.

_____. More on The Gentle Art of Verbal Self-Defense. Englewood Cliffs, NJ: Prentice-Hall, Inc., 1983.

Ellickson, J.L. "The Effect of Interviewers Responding Differentially to Subjects' Representational Systems as Indicated by Eye Movement." (Doctoral dissertation, Michigan State University, 1980.) Dissertation Abstracts International. (1981) 41(7): 2754B.

_____. "Representational Systems and Eye Movements in an Interview." Journal of Counseling Psychology. (1983): 30, 339-345.

Ellis, J.L. "Representation Systems: An Investigation of Sensory Predicate Use in a Self-Disclosure Interview." (Doctoral dissertation, University of Minnesota, 1980.) Dissertation Abstracts International. (1981) 41(11): 4244B.

Evans, Frederick J. "Contextual Forgetting: Posthypnotic Source Amnesia." Journal of Abnormal Psychology. (1979) 88(5): 556-563.

Falzett, W.C. "Matched Versus Unmatched Primary Representational Systems and the Relationship to Perceived Trustworthiness in a Counseling Analogue." (Doctoral dissertation, Marquette University, 1979.) Dissertation Abstracts International. (1980) 41(1): 105A.

_____. "Matched Versus Unmatched Primary Representational Systems and the Relationship to Perceived Trustworthiness in a Counseling Analogue." Journal of Counseling Psychology. (1981): 28, 305-308.

Faris, G.J. "Psychologic Aspects of Athletic Rehabilitation." Clinics in Sports Medicine. (July, 1985) 4(3): 545-551.

Farmer, S.S. "Supervisory Conferences in Communicative Disorders: Verbal and Non-verbal Interpersonal Communication Pacing." (Doctoral dissertation, University of Colorado at Boulder.) Dissertation Abstracts International. (1984) 44(9): 27815B.

Farrelly, Frank and Jeff Brandsma. Provocative Therapy. Cupertino, CA: Meta Publications, Inc., 1974.

Feldman, Dot, and Kay Grask. "NLP and Family Therapy." Presented at AAMFT, Washington, D.C., October 6, 1983.

Ferguson, M. "NLP: A Science for Increasing 'Beneficial Choices.'" Brain Mind Bulletin. (June 21, 1982): 7(11), 1-3.

Frieden, Frederick Paul. "Speaking the Client's Language: The Effects of Neuro-Linguistic Programming (Predicate Matching) on Verbal and Nonverbal Behaviors in Psychotherapy -- A Single Case Design." Dissertation Abstracts International. (1981) 42(3): 1171B.

Fromme, D.K., and J. Daniell. "NLP Examined: Imagery, Sensory Mode, and Communication." Journal of Counseling Psychology. (1984): 31(3), 387-390.

Frye, Mary Lois. "Analysis of the Relationship Between Leisure Interests and Representational Systems Among College Freshmen Students With Implications for Leisure Counseling." (Doctoral dissertation, Oklahoma State University, 1980.) Dissertation Abstracts International: 4106A:2764.

Gardner, F.M. "What's That You Say? Eyes Have the Answer." The Oregonian. March 15, 1982.

Garmston, R.J. "Book Reviews: Master Teaching Techniques by Bernard F. Cleveland." National Staff Development Council. (December 1985): 2,6.

Gehlbach, Roger D. "Individual Differences: Implications for Instructional Theory, Research, and Innovation." Review of Education Research: 49(2), 8-14.

Gilligan, S.G. "Ericksonian Approaches to Clinical Hypnosis." Ericksonian Approaches to Hypnosis and Psythotherapy. J. Zweig (ed). New York: Brunner/Mazel, (1982): 87-103

Goleman, Daniel. "People Who Read People." Psychology Today. (July 1979): 66.

Gordon, David. Therapeutic Metaphors: Helping Others Through the Looking Glass. Cupertino, CA: Meta Publications, 1978.

_____. "Ericksonian Anecdotal Therapy." Ericksonian Approaches to Hypnosis and Psychotherapy. J. Zweig (ed). New York: Bunner/Mazel, 1982: 114-119.

Gordon, D. and M. Meyers-Anderson. Phoenix: Therapeutic Patterns of Milton H. Erickson. Cupertino, CA: Meta Publications, 1982.

Graunke, B.R. "An Evaluation of Neurolinguistic Programming, the Impact of Varied Imaging Tasks Upon Sensory Predicates." Dissertation Abstracts International. (December 1984) 45(6): 19120B.

Green, Margaret Ann. "Trust as Effected by Representational System Predicates." (Doctoral dissertation, Ball State University, 1979.) Dissertation Abstracts International. (1981) 41(8): 3159B.

Greenberg, George and Deborah Zeigler, "Getting Fired: Crisis and Opportunity in Midlife" Voices/A Journal Published Quarterly. American Academy of Psychotherapists. (Spring, 1982): 66-73.

Gregory, Peter B. "NLP Techniques Applied to the Treatment of Vietnam Combat Veteran Suffering from Symptoms of PTSD, A Case Study." Med. Service VAM % ROC For Harrison, Mt. 1985 (published as an appendix in Magic In Action by Richard Bandler. Cupertino, CA: Meta Publications.

Griffith, N. "The Charismatic Kid." Life. (March, 1985) V.8, No. 3: 42.

Grinder, John, and Richard Bandler. The Structure of Magic II. Palo Alto, CA: Science and Behavior Books, 1976.

_____. Trance-Formations: Neuro-Linguistic Programming and the Structure of Hypnosis. Moab, UT: Real People Press, 1981.

_____. Reframing: Neuro-Linguistic Programming and the Transformation of Meaning. Moab, UT: Real People Press, 1982.

Grinder, J., R. Bandler, and J. DeLozier. Patterns of Hypnotic Techniques of Milton H. Erickson (Vol. 2). Cupertino, CA: Meta Publications, 1977.

Grinder, J., and M. D. McMaster. "Use an 'Outcome Frame' to Produce Results." Successful Meetings. (March 1981): 99.

Grzebieniak, J.F. "The Relationship Between Selected Jungian Personality Types as Determined on the Myers-Briggs Type Indicator and Their Use ofSensory Referenced Predicates as Described by Bandler and Grinder." Dissertation Abstracts International. (October 1983) 44(4): 989-000-A.

Gullerud, Ernest N. "Washington University Cognitive Representational Systems: A Conceptual Analysis of Developmental Trends Anticipated in Cognitive Structures Designed to Interpret Man's Reality." Dissertation Abstracts International. (1971) 32/04A:2198.

Gunn, Scout Lee, Adventures in Excellence. Stillwater, OK: Excellence Unlimited.

_____. The Excellence Principle: Utilizing NLP. Stillwater, OK: Excellence Unlimited.

_____. "Meta Communication: Leisure Counseling That Looks Behind Defenses", Parks and Recreation. (15)5: 74-76, 83.

_____. Leisure Counseling Using NLP. Stillwater, OK: International Society of Leisure Therapies, 1981.

_____. "Neurolinguistic Programming: A New Horizon in Leisure Counseling." Therapeutic Recreation Journal. Vol. XV, 4th Quarter (4). (1981): 36-43.

Hagstrom, G. "Microanalysis of Direct Confrontation Psychotherapy with Schizophrenics: Using Neurolinguistic Programming and Delsarte's System of Expression." (Doctoral dissertation, California School of Professional Psychology, 1981.) Dissertation Abstracts International. (1982) 42(10): 4192B.

Haley, M.C. "The Eyes Have It." Real Estate Today. (February 1982): 24.

Hammer, A.L. "Language as a Therapeutic Tool: The Effects on the Relationship of Listeners Responding to Speakers by Using Perceptual Predicates." Dissertation Abstracts International. (September 1980,): 41(3).

_____. "Matching Perceptual Predicates: Effect on Perceived Empathy in a Counseling Analogue." Journal of Counseling Psychology. (1983): 30, 172-179.

Hampton-Turner, C. "The Linguistics of Therapy: Noam Chomsky, Richard Bandler and John Grinder." Maps of the Mind. New York: Ollier Books, 1981.

Hansen, James, C., Ronald E. Pound, and Richard W. Warner, Jr. "Use of Modeling Procedures."

Harman, Robert L., and Charles O'Neill. "Neuro-Linguistic Programming for Counselors." Personnel and Guidance Journal. (March 1981): 499.

Harper, Linda. Classroom Magic -- Effective Teaching Made Easy, Troy, MI, Twigg Communications, 1982.

Haskell, P. "NLP and Transformation: A Conversation with Michael McMaster." Houston, TX: RHA.

Haynie, Nancy Ann. "Systematic Human Relations Training With Neuro-Linguistic Programming." (Doctoral dissertation, University of Georgia, 1981.).

Hegarty, Christopher and Charlotte Bretto. "How to Build High Levels of Rapport." Santa Cruz, CA: The Center for Professional Development, 1987.

Hernandez, Vivian Ofelia. "A Study of Eye Movement Patterns in the Neurolinguistic Programming Model." (Doctoral dissertation, Ball State University, 1981.) Dissertation Abstracts International. (1981) 42(4): 1587B.

Hill, E.L. "An Empirical Test of the NLP Concept of Anchoring" Dissertation Abstracts International. (June 1984) 44(7): 2246B.

Hillin, H.H. "Effects of a Rapport Method and Chemical Dependency Workshop of Adults Employed in Kansas Service Agencies." Dissertation Abstracts International. (June 1984) 44(12): 3574A.

Howe, Michael J.A. Adult Learning: Psychological Research and Applications. New York: John Wiley and Sons.

Hupp, D. "Neuro-Linguistic Programming and Unconscious Learning." Pathways. (Available from the NLP Institute of D.C.). (Fall 1981).

Hupp, D., and T. T. Singh. "Meta Programming and Family Therapy." The Family Therapy Networker. (1982): 6(6), 28-31.

Hutchinson, M. "Is NLP Really Magic? An Interview with Leslie Cameron-Bandler." Wisconsin Counselor. (Spring 1982): 23.

Jacobson, Sid. Meta-Cation: Prescriptions for Some Ailing Educational Processes. Cupertino, CA: Meta Publications, 1983.

_____. "New Model Developed for Total Communication." Business & Industry Coordinator Magazine. (Winter 1985): 57.

_____. "Consulting, Writing, and the Business of Business." The Professional Writing Consultant. (Fall 1986): 1.

_____. Meta-Cation, Vol. II: New Improved Formulas For Thinking About Thinking. Cupertino, CA: META Publications, 1986.

_____. Meta-Cation, Vol. III: Powerful Applications For Strong Relief. Cupertino, CA: META Publications, 1986.

Janees, T. and W. Woodsmall, W. Time Line Therapy And the Basis of Personality.

Jepsen, C. "Behavioral Management of Dental Fear, Anxiety, and Phobia." A Correspondence Course for Dentist, XVII. (1986): 29-36.

_____. "Precision Communication." Health Caring. (1986): 1(2), 2.

Johannsen, Clifford A. "Predicates, Mental Imagery in Discrete Sense Modes, and Levels of Stress: The NLP Typologies." (United States International University, Psych., Clinical, 1982.) Dissertation Abstracts International. 43(8): 2709B.

Kendig, F. "Listening to Radar." Psychology Today. (1982) 16(12): 80.

King, Mark, Larry Novik, and Charles Citrenbaum. Irresistible Communication: Creative Skills for the Health Professional. Philadelphia, PA: W.B. Saunders, Co., 1983.

Knowles, Ruth Dailey. "Building Rapport Through Neuro-Linguistic Programming." American Journal of Nursing. (July 1983): 1011-4.

_____. A Guide to Self-Management Strategies for Nurses. New York: Springer Publishing Co., 1984.

Korzybski, A. Science and Sanity. Lakeville, CN: The International Non-Aristotelian Library Publishing Company, 4th Edition, 1933.

Kraft, W.A. "The Effects of Primary Representational System Congruence on Relaxation in a Neurolinguistic Programming Model." (Doctoral dissertation, Texas A & M University, 1982.) Dissertation Abstracts International. (1982) 43(70): 2372B.

Krakauer, J. "Neuro-Linguistic Programming." Ultrasport. (July 1986): 21-23.

Krier, B.A. "Fire-Walking 'Hot Trend'." The Cleveland Plain Dealer. (May 7, 1984): D1. (Reprinted for the Los Angeles Times).

Kuhn, T.S. The Structure of Scientific Revolutions. University of Chicago Press, 1970.

Laborde, Genie Z. "Neuro-Linguistic Programming." New Realities. (1982): 4(1), 8.

_____. "Don't Eat the Menu." New Realities. (1982b): 4(4), 14.

_____. Influencing with Integrity. Palo Alto, CA: Syntony Inc. Publishing Co., 1983.

_____. 90 Days to Communication Excellence. Palo Alto, CA: Syntony Publishing, 1985.

_____. Fine Tune Your Brain. Palo Alto, CA: Syntony Publishing, 1988.

Laborde, G.Z., and B. Dillman. "The Structure of Charisma: Playing with Power and Matches." New Realities. (1982): 4(4), 8.

Lange, D.E. "A Validity Study of the Construct 'Most Highly Valued Representational System' in Human Auditory and Visual Perceptions." (Doctoral dissertation, Louisiana State University, 1980.) Dissertation Abstracts International. (1981) 41(11): 4266B.

Lankton, Stephen R. Practical Magic: The Clinical Applications of Neuro-Linguistic Programming. Cupertino, CA: Meta Publications, 1979.

Lankton, S.R., C. H. Lankton, and M. Brown. "Psychological Level Communication in Transactional Analysis." The Transactional Analysis Journal. (1981): 11, 287-298.

Lauerman, C. "Seeing, Hearing, Smelling: Sensible Therapy." Chicago Tribune. (March 13, 1985) 2 : 1, 4.

Lee, Scout, Brooke Medicine Eagle and Jan Summers. The Challenge of Excellence, Vol 1 Learning the Ropes of Change. Stillwater, OK: Excellence Unlimited.

Leffel, Gary Michael. "The Role of Metaphor in Human Behavior." Graduation with Distinction Project. Point Loma College, 1977.

Leo, J. "Reprogramming the Patient." Time. (December 19, 1983): 79.

Lewis, Byron A. and L. Marvell-Mell. The NLP Skill Builders Book 1: Basic Techniques in NLP. Lake Oswego, OR: Metamorphous Press.

Lewis, Byron A. and R. Frank Pucelik. Magic Demystified: A Pragmatic Guide to Communication and Change. Lake Oswego, OR: Metamorphous Press, 1982.

Liberman, M.B. "The Treatment of Simple Phobias with NLP Techniques." Dissertation Abstracts International. (December 1984) 45(6): 1918B.

Liggett, K.R. "The Effects of a Linguistic Training Model and Counselor Conceptual Complexity on Counseling Skills." (Doctoral dissertation, University of Nebraska at Lincoln, 1977) Dissertation Abstracts International. (1978) 38(8): 3853B.

Linden, A. and F. Stass. A Handbook for Basic Neuto-Linguistic Programming Training. New York: New York Training Institute for Neuro-Linguistic Programming, 1985.

Lucas, B.A. "The Effectiveness of Unimodal vs. Bimodal Sensory Feedback for the Males and Females in a Finger Temperature Training Task." (Doctoral dissertation, Kansas State University, 1979.) Dissertation Abstracts International. (1980) 41(1): 399B.

Ludwig, J. and D. Menendez. Effective Communication through Neurolinguistics. Training and Development Journal. (March 1985): 44, 46, 48.

Lunde, T. "NLP (Neuro-Linguistic Programming) and Graphology." American Handwriting Analysis Foundation News. (July, 1982) 15(4):1,3.

Mace, S. "The Eyes Have It: NLP Learning Theories Inspire Spelling Program." InfoWorld. (March 22, 1982): 8.

_____. "Neuro-Linguistic Programming Breeds Software." InfoWorld. (1983) 5(8): 15.

MacLean, Mary. "The Neurolinguistic Programming Model." In Francis J. Turner (ed.). Social Work Treatment. The Free Press. (1987): 341-375.

Macroy, T.D. "Linguistic Surface Structure in Family Interaction." (Doctoral dissertation, Utah State University, 1978.) Dissertation Abstracts International. (1979) 40(2): 926B.

Marcus, Eric H. "Neurolinguistic Programming." Personnel Journal. (December 1983): 972-8.

Marvell-Mell, Linnea. Basic Techniques in NLP: Book 1. Lake Oswego, OR: Metamorphous Press.

Mason, D. "Neurolinguistic Programming: The Answer to Change?" Training and Development Journal. (1979): 33 (10), 68.

Mather, B.D. "The Effect of Representational Predicates on Relaxation." Dissertation Abstracts International. (1983) 44(4): 1222B.

Mathes, L. Rapport: A Workbook. Vienna, VA: NLP of Washington D.C., 1982.

Mattar, A. T. "The Validity of Neurolinguistic Programming's Auditory Primary Representational System." (Unpublished Masters Thesis, Utah State University, 1980.).

_____. "Primary Representational Systems as a Basis for Improved Comprehension and Communication." (Doctoral dissertation, Utah State University, 1980.) Dissertation Abstracts International. (1981) 41(8): 3162B.

May, Rollo J. Journal of Human Psychology. 16(4):33-51.

McAllister, M. "New Process Cuts Therapy From Years to Minutes." The Sunday Camera. (June 10, 1979): 57.

McCarthy, W.J. and B.J. Leikind. "Walking on Fire: Feat of Mind?" Psychology Today. (February 1986).

McCormick, D. M. "Primary Representational Systems and Satir Coping Styles." Unpublished paper. The University of California at Santa Cruz, 1975.

_____. "Neurolinguistic Programming: A Resource Guide and Review of the Research." In L.D. Goodstein and J.W. Pfeiffer (eds.). The 1984 Annual: Developing Human Resources. San Diego, CA: University Associates: 267-281

McCoy, R. "Innovative System: Results with Disabled Children Astonish Educators, Parents." Rocky Mountain News. (May 26, 1981): 40.

McIntosh, B. "The Case of the Rip-Off Romeo." West. (November 17, 1985).

McMaster, Michael D "NLP and Transformation: A Conversation with Michael McMaster". Houston, TX: RHA.

_____. Creating The Conditions for Results, Lake Oswego, OR: Metamorphous Press.

McMaster, M.D., and J. Grinder. Precision: A New Approach to Communication (High Quality Information Processing for Business). Los Angeles: Precision, 1980.

_____. "The Art of Communicating." Administrative Management. (1980): 41, 56.

Mercier, M. "Relation of Therapist-Client Predicates to Client Satisfaction." (Unpublished. The University of Pennsylvania, 1982.) Write M.A. Mercier, Dept. of Psychiatry, 1725 W. Harrison, Suite 1084, St. Lukes Medical Center, Chicago, IL 60612.

Mercier, M.A., and M. Johnson. "Representational System Predicate Use and Covergence in Counseling: Gloria Revisited." Journal of Counseling Psychology. (1984): 31, 161-169.

Meskin, Bonnie B., and Jerome L. Singer. "Daydreaming, Reflective Thought, and Laterality of Eye Movements." Journal of Personality and Social Psychology. (1974): 30(1), 64-71.

Miller, G. "The Magical Number Seven, Plus or Minus Two." Psychology Review, Volume 83, 1957.

Miller, G., E. Galanter, and K. Pribram. Plans and the Structure of Behavior. New York, NY: Henry Holt and Company, Inc., 1960.

Moine, Donald J. "Patterns of Persuasion." Personal Selling Power. (1981): 1 (4), 3.

_____. "A Psycholinguistic Study of the Patterns of Persuasion Used by Successful Salespeople." (Doctoral dissertation, University of Oregon, 1981.) Dissertation Abstracts International. 42(5): 2135B.

_____. "To Trust, Perchance to Buy." Psychology Today. (August 1982) 50-54.

Moine, Donald J., and John H. Herd. "Neuro-Linguistic Sales Programming: The Unfair Advantage." Personal Selling Power. (July-August 1983): 6-7.

_____. Modern Persuasion Strategies: The Hidden Advantage in Selling. Englewood Cliffs, NJ: Prentice Hall, Inc., 1984.

Moran, S. with D. Kaplan. "Tony Robbins: Firewalking for Fun and Profit." Bay Guardian, San Francisco) (Dec. 4,1985).

Morris, F.R., and D. G. Morris. The Meta System. South Bend, IN: Center for Creative Change, undated.

Newman, E. "Now for a Leak in Doublespeak." The Cleveland Plain Dealer, (March 17, 1982): 19A. (Reprinted from the New York Times.).

Oliver, B. "Powerful Patterns of Persuasion." The Toastmaster. (March 1982): 25-27.

Owens, L.F. "An Investigation of Eye Movements and Representational Systems." (Doctoral dissertation, Ball State University, 1977.) Dissertation Abstracts International. (1978) 38(10): 4992B.

Pantin, H.M. "The Relationship Between Subjects' Predominant Sensory Predicate Use, Their Preferred Representational System and Self-Reported Attitudes Towards Similar Versus Different Therapist-Patient Dyads." (Doctoral dissertation, University of Miami, 1982.) Dissertation Abstracts International. (1983) 43(7): 2350B.

Paubeckas, A.J. "Rapport in the Therapeutic Relationship and Its Relationship to Pacing." Dissertation Abstracts International. (December 1981) 42(6): 2543-4B.

Paxton, L.D. "Representational Systems and Client Perception of the Counseling Relationship." (Doctoral dissertation, Indiana University, 1980.) Dissertation Abstracts International. (1981) 41(9): 3888A.

Perry, Campbell, Robert Gelfand and Phillip Marcovitch. "The Relevance of Hypnotic Susceptibility in the Clinical Context." Journal of Abnormal Psychology. (1979) 88(5): 592-603.

Pribram, K. The Language of the Brain. Englewood Cliffs, NJ: Prentice Hall, 1971.

Pucelik, R.F. The META Handbook: Basic Principles of Communication and Change. Cupertino, CA: META Publications.

Pulvino, Charles, James Lee, and Cynthia Forman. Communications with Clients: A Guide for Financial Professional. Prentice Hall, Englewood Cliffs, NJ, 1987.

Rapaport, Anatol, Ed. General Systems Yearbooks. Washington, DC: Society for General Systems Research.

Rebstock, M.E. "The Effects of Training in Matching Techniques on the Development of Rapport Between Client and Counselor During Initial Counseling Interviews." (Doctoral dissertation, University of Missouri at Kansas City, 1980.) Dissertation Abstracts International. (1980) 41(3): 946A.

Rhinelander, Phillip H. Is Man Comprehensible to Man? Stanford, CA: Stanford Alumni Association, 1973.

Richardson, J., and J. Margoulis. The Magic of Rapport. San Francisco: Harbor, 1981.

Robbins, Anthony. Unlimited Power. New York: Simon and Schuster, 1986.

Rule, W.R. "Family Therapy and the Pie Metaphor." Journal of Marital and Family Therapy. (1983): 9(1), 101-103.

Rushefsky, C. "Don't Give Up on the Slient Type too Soon." The Cleveland Plain Dealer. (October 21, 1984): 14. (Syndicated through Newhouse News Service).

Russell, D. "The Firewalk Experience...Fear into Power". The Movement: An Exploration of Inner Awareness. (February 1984) 9(2): 6-7.

Ruthlow, J. "Hypnosis: Unseen Edge in Top Sales." Los Angeles Times. (April 15, 1982) Section IX: 1-3.

Saltmarsh and M. Rawlins. Illinois Guidance and Personnel Quarterly. (Spring).

Sandu, Daya Singh. "The Effects of Mirroring vs. Non-Mirroring of Clients' Nonverbal Behaviors on Empathy, Trustworthiness, and Positive Interaction in Cross-Cultural Counseling Dyads." (Doctoral dissertation, Mississippi State University, 1984.) Dissertation Abstracts International. (1984) 45(4): 1042A.

Sarbin, Theodore R., and William C. Coe. "Hypnosis and Psychopathology: Replacing Old Myths With Fresh Metaphors." Journal of Abnormal Psychology. (1979) 88(5): 506-526.

Satir, Virginia. Conjoint Family Therapy. Palo Alto: Science and Behavior Books, 1964.

_____. Peoplemaking. Palo Alto: Science and Behavior Books, 1972.

Schmedien, G.W. "The Impact of Sensory Modality Matching on the Establishments of Rapport in Psychotherapy." (Doctoral dissertation, Kent State University, 1981.) Dissertation Abstracts International. (1981) 42(3): 2080B.

Schneider, Mark Edward. "The Relationship Among Primary Representational Systems, and Counselor Empathy, Trustworthiness, Attractiveness, Expertness and Subject Preference." (Doctoral dissertation, State University of New York at Buffalo, 1984.) Dissertation Abstracts International. (August 1984) 45(2): 418A.

Schoen, S. "NLP: An Overview." Psychotherapy Newsletter. (1983) 1(1), 16-25.

Schwid, B. Communicating with clients NLP and handwriting. American Handwriting Analysis Foundation News. (July) 14(4):1,3,4.

Sharpely, C.F. "Predicate Matching in NLP: A Review of Research on the Preferred Representational System." Journal of Counseling Psychology, 31: 238-248.

Shaw, D.L. "Recall as Affected by the Interaction of Presentation Representational System and Primary Representational System." (Doctoral dissertation, Ball State University, 1977.) Dissertation Abstracts International. (1978) 38(10): 5931A.

Shobin, M.A. "An Investigation of the Effect of Verbal Pacing on Initial Therapeutic Rapport." (Doctoral dissertation, University of Boston.) Dissertation Abstracts International. (November 1980) 41(5): 1960A.

Slavit, M.R. "The Effects of Assessing and Utilizing Preferred Sensory Modality: An Experiment With Relaxation Training." (Doctoral dissertation, University of Texas at Austin, 1983.) Dissertation Abstracts International. (1984) 44(9): 2907B.

Smith, Lawrence and Loretta Malandro. Courtroom Communication Strategies. New York: Kluwer Law Book Publishers, Inc., 1985.

Snow, Richard E. "Individual Differences and Instructional Theory."

Society of Neuro-Linguistic Programming. Directory of Practitioners, Master Practitioners and Trainers, 1982. Santa Cruz, CA: Not Ltd., 1982.

Spear, J.H. "On the road again: A mental health map to the mainstreamed hearing impaired." Volta Review. (September 1984) 86: 3.

Sperber, K. "The Language of Empathy." Dissertation Abstracts International. (August 1984) 45(2): 688B.

Stefano, Steven and Charlotte Bretto. "Analogies for Training Technical Information." Santa Cruz, CA: The Center for Professional Development, 1986.

Stevens, B. "Gestalt and Neurolinguistic Programming." The Gestalt Journal. (1978) 1(2), 89-91.

Stevens, J.O. "Neuro-Linguistic Programming (NLP) and Gestalt." The Gestalt Journal. (1978): 8, 1(2), 83-88.

_____. "Neuro-Linguistic Programming." In R. Herink, Ed.. The Psychotherapy Handbook. New York: New American Library, 1980.

Stone, Christopher. Re-Creating Your Self. Portland, OR: Metamorphous Press, 1988.

Sullivan, R. "What Makes a Man Irresistible? Ask the Wives and Lovers of Andrew Afar." Redbook. (June 1986): 94, 95, 144-8.

Taylor, C.L. "Reading Non-Verbal Cues: A Key to Manager-Employee Rapport?" Los Angeles Business Journal. (September 15, 1980): 423-425.

Taylor, R. "Anthony Robbins...Experiencing Success." The Movement: An Exploration of Inner Awareness. (February) 9(2): 6-7.

The, L. "Self-Improvement: Beyond Productivity." Personal Computing. (July 1982): 89.

Thomason, David Dallas. "Neurolinguistic Programming: An Aid to Increase Counselor Expertness." (Rosemead School of Psychology, 1984.) Dissertation Abstracts International. (1984) 44(9): 2909B.

Thomason, T.C., T. Arbuckle and D. Cody. "Test of the eye-movement hypothesis of neurolinguistic programming." Perceptual and Motor Skills. (1980): 51, 230.

Thweatt, W.H. "Effective Permission-Giving and Representational Systems." Transactional Analysis Journal. (1980): 10(1), 53-55.

Til, L. "Book Review of Modern Persuasion Strategies by Moine & Herd." Sales Report. 1(4): 29.

Tobin, B.A. "The Roles of Modeling Theory and Transformational Grammar in the Development of a Theory of Verbal Intervention in Psychotherapy: A Critical Analysis of Bandler and Grinder's 'The Structure of Magic.'" Dissertation Abstracts International. (1984) 44(9): 2795A.

Torres, C. "An Investigation of Language Representational System by Personality Type." Dissertation Abstracts International. (November 1984) 45(5): 1271A.

Vaihinger, H. The Philosophy of "As If". London, England: Routliedge, Kegan and Paul, Ltd., 1924.

Vallance, K. "Hypnotic Techniques Gain Acceptance in Business World." The Christian Science Monitor. (October 28, 1982): 6.

Vallance, L. "Hypnotic Techniques Move Into Worlds of Selling, Education." Portland, OR: Oregonian. (November 5, 1982).

Vander, Z. "The Effects of Meta-Model Questioning and Empathic Responding on Concreteness in Client Statements and Client Ratings of Anxiety and Counselor Attractiveness, Expertness, and Trustworthiness." Dissertation Abstracts International. (June 1984) 44(12): 3600-3601A.

Varven, J. "The Schoolhouse Apple." Softalk. (May 1982): 36.

Waters, C. "Richard Bandler: Epistemological Magician." Santa Cruz Express. (January 21, 1982): 6.

Wilimek, J.F. "The Use of Language Representational Systems By High and Low Marital Adjustment Couples." (Doctoral dissertation, The University of Utah, 1979.) Dissertation Abstracts International. (1980) 40(7): 3914A.

Wood, W. "For Them, Mind, Body are Part of the Same Thing." Santa Cruz Sentinel. (August 1977): 25.

Yakin, M. "Multiplier Method Algorithms for Inequality Constrained NLP Problems." (University of Michigan, Engineering.) Industrial Dissertation Abstracts International, 42/02-B: 718.

Yapko, M.D. "Neuro-Linguistic Programming, Hypnosis, and Interpersonal Influence." (Doctoral dissertation, United States International University, 1980.) Dissertation Abstracts International, 1981, 41(8): 3204B.

_____. "The Effect of Matching Primary Representational System Predicates on Hypnotic Relaxation." The American Journal of Clinical Hypnosis, 1981, 23, 169-175.

_____. "A Comparative Analysis of Direct and Indirect Hypnotic Communication Styles." American Journal of Clinical Hypnosis, (1983): 25, 270-5.

_____. "Implications of the Ericksonian and Neurolinguistic Programming approaches for Responsibility of Therapeutic Outcomes." American Journal of Clinical Hypnosis. (1984): 27, 137-43.

Yeager, Joseph. A Collection of Management Articles Related to NLP. Princeton, NJ: Eastern NLP Institute.

_____. Thinking About Thinking With NLP. Cupertino, CA: Meta Publications, 1985

York, Robert J. "Effects of Hypnosis on Motivation, Memory, and Concentration and as an Adjunct to a Low Achiever's Study Habits." Hypnosis. (1981): 25(2).

Zemke, R. "Neurolinguistic Programming." Training/HRD. (December, 1979): 87.

Zientara, M., "IBMer Tells How to Handle a Prima Donna." Compterworld. (November 15, 1982): 13.

GLOSSARY

GLOSSARY

Accessing Cues - External behaviors that indicate how a person is processing information internally.

Anchoring - The process of associating an internal response with some external trigger (similar to classical conditioning) so that the response may be quickly, and sometimes covertly, accessed.

Associated - actually experienceing the feelings (emotions), along with the sights, sounds, tastes and/or smells of an event - whether that event is occurring in the present, remembered from the past, or totally constructed.

Attention - The intentional channeling of awareness.

Behavior - All sensory representations experienced and expressed internally and/or externally for which evidence is available from a subject and/or from a human observer of that subject.

Behavioral Flexibility - The ability to vary one's own behavior in order to elicit or secure a response from another person.

Calibrated Loop - Unconscious pattern of communication in which behavioral cues of one person trigger specific responses from another person in an on-going interaction.

Calibration - The ability to notice and measure changes with respect to a standard. Calibration depends on refined sensory acuity. You probably have a good idea of when a loved one is feeling a little unsure or very happy. This is because you have calibrated what their physiology means.

Communication - The process of the transfer of information by language, signs, symbols, and behavior.

Congruity / Incongruity - A situation in which the message a person communicates is the same/similar, or different/dissimilar, respectively, in all output channels - that is, the words of the message convey the same meaning as the tone of voice, and the gestures convey the same meaning as the previous two. All output channels are being aligned. Incongruency exhibits conflicting messages between output channels. Example: saying, "Yes, I'm sure!" in a soft, querulous voice.

Control - The process by means of which a whole entity retains its identity and/or performance under changing circumstances.

Cybernetics - A formal way of discussing epistemological processes and methods of change which views a symptom as part of the organizational logic of its ecology. Formally, cybernetics refers to the entire field of control and communication theory, whether in machine or animal, in so far as behaviors are regular, determinate, or reproducible.

Cybernetic theory - is essentially a meta-model (a model about modeling). Cybernetic models are different from statistical or linear models in that they deal with the feedback of total systems, systems in which events at any position in the system may be expected to have effect at all postions in the system at later times. In cybernetic models, a particular cause or effect cannot be isolated from its context. Therefore, each function must be considered and measured in terms of the whole. Human behavior and experience are undoubtedly the result of such a system. Therefore any satisfactory model of human experience, behavioral, physiological or epistemological, must be cybernetic. For more on this see pages 21-33, Roots of NLP, Dilts (1983) and/or Steps to an Ecology of Mind, Bateson (1972).

Deep Structure - The sensory maps (both conscious and unconscious) that people use to organize and guide their behavior.

Deletion - What there was in original experience that has been left out of internal representation. This is one of the cognitive processes that keeps us from being overwhelmed by incoming sensory data. There are things we leave out, however, that would on occasion be much more useful for us to include.

Distortion - The process by which things are inaccurately included in a person's internal representation in some way that limits him/her. It could be "blown out of proportion," "twisted a bit," and the like. It allows us to shift our sensory data.

Ecology - A concern for the totality or pattern of relationships between a being and its environment. In NLP we also use the term in reference to internal ecology, the pattern of values, strategies, and behaviors a person embodies in relationship to himself/herself.

Elicitation - The procedure used to gather the necessary information to make explicit the ordered sequence of representational system activity that constitutes a particular strategy.

Emergent Properties - The principle that whole entities exhibit properties which are meaningful only when attributed to the whole, not to its parts.

Epistemology - A study of the means by which we acquire and express knowledge of the world.

Eye-Scanning Patterns - A particular set of accessing cues based on how the eyes move and the sequence of positions they move to. Knowing which internal process each position correlates to is the precursor to understanding and eliciting strategies.

Frame - The context in which information is transmitted or perceived, a state of mind.

Future Pacing - The process of mentally rehearsing some future situation in order to help ensure that the desired behavior will occur naturally and automatically in that situation.

Generalization - The cognitive process by which parts of internal experience are separated from the original experience and become a class of their own. In many cases this is useful. For example, a child has an experience of touching a stove top and getting slightly burned. He may generalize to "Burners are hot" or "Don't touch stoves when they're on." In other cases it can limit a person's model of the world in nonuseful ways.

Hierarchy - The principle according to which entities meaningfully treated as wholes are built up of smaller entities which are themselves wholes, and so on. In a hierarchy emergent properties denote the levels.

Internal Representation - The configuration of information you create, store and recall in your mind in the form of pictures, sounds, feelings, smells, and tastes. To "recall" what the house you grew up in looked like, unless you are actually there, you remember an internal representation.

Map - A drawing or other composite representation of the information available about how the world really is or operates.

Matching - Adopting parts of another person's behavior, such as particular gestures, facial expressions, forms of speech, tone of voice, etc. Done subtly, it helps create a feeling of rapport between people.

Meta-model - A representation of a representation. For example, language is a representation of the world of experience; transformational grammar is a representation of language and, therefore, a Meta-model.

Mirroring - Adopting other people's behaviors as though you were a "mirror image." If you were facing someone who had his left hand on his cheek, you would put your right hand on your cheek in the same way.

Model - An intellectual construct of an entity, in which at least one observer has an interest. The observer may wish to relate his model and, if appropriate its mechanisms, to observables in the world. When this is done it frequently leads - understandably, but not accurately - to descriptions of the world constructed in terms of models, as if the world were identical with models of it.

Modeling - The process of identifying patterns in the interaction between human behavior and the environment, so that the behavior of individual human beings can be systematized within selected contexts to achieve desired and adaptive outcomes more efficiently, effectively and consistently.

Outcomes - Results or desired states that a person or organization aspires to achieve.

Pacing - Matching the behavior, beliefs, mood, or interests of another person to achieve rapport.

Problem Situation - A nexus of real-world events and ideas which is problematic and for which other possibilities concerning the situation are worth investigating.

Process - The elements in a problem situation which are characterized by continuous change.

Rapport - The phenomenon of people trading and/or sharing particular behaviors which happens naturally and unconsciously as people spend time together and can be done purposefully, by mirroring and matching.

Representational Systems - Internal information processing system using a particular sensory modality. Visual, auditory, kinesthetic, olfactory, and gustatory, enable us to take in and store information, sort it, and use it. The distinctions we make as human beings (internally and externally) come to us through these systems.

Secondary Gain - Where some seemingly negative or problematic behavior actually carries out some positive function at some other level. For example, drinking may help a person relax or help them fit a particular self-image (identity).

Sensory Awareness - The process of refining our ability to make distinctions among the visual, auditory, kinesthetic, olfactory, and gustatory systems. This gives us fuller, richer sensory experiences and the ability to create detailed, sensory-based descriptions from our interaction with the external world.

Sensory-based Description - Using words that convey information that is directly observable, verifiable, by the five senses. It is the difference between "Her lips are pulled taut, some parts of her teeth are showing, the edges of her mouth are higher than the main line of her mouth" and "She's happy."

Sensory-based Experience - An experience that is processed on the level of what can be seen, heard, felt, smelled, and/or tasted.

State - The sum total of all neurological processes within an individual at any one moment in time, which filters or affects the final result of interpretation of any experience at that moment.

Strategy - A systematically ordered sequence of (usually all) sensory representations. A strategy usually includes each of the sensory representational systems (visual, auditory, kinesthetic) in some order. We can discover them in ourselves and in others by listening to the words we choose, observing eye-scanning patterns, and asking about the form and sequence of internal representations.

Structural Elements - The "building blocks" of a model.

Submodalities - The subclassifications of external and internal sensory experience: a picture has brightness, distance, depth. Sounds have volume, location, tone, and so forth.

Surface Structure - The words or linguistic representations used to describe or stand for the actual primary sensory representations stored in the brain.

Synesthesia - The process of overlap between any two representational systems, characterized by phenomena like "see-feel circuits," in which a person derives feelings from what he sees, and "hear-feel circuits," in which a person gets feelings from what he hears. Any two sensory modalities may be linked together.

Syntax - The set of rules or directives that describe how the structural elements of a model may be put together. Within language, the study of the order and patterning of words and phrases.

System - A model of a whole entity. When applied to human activity, the model is characterized fundamentally in terms of hierarchical structure, emergent properties, communication, and control.

Territory - Used to refer to the "real" world, as opposed to the world as we perceive it.

TOTE - Developed by Miller, Galanter and Pribram (1960), the term stands for the sequence Test - Operate-Test-Exit, which describes the basic feedback loop used to guide all behavior.

Transderivational Search - The process of searching back through one's stored mental representations to find the reference experience from which a current behavior or response derives.

Utilization - The process of applying an existing elicited strategy, for the purpose of assisting a client (individual, family, group or organization) in achieving some desired outcome, or securing some outcome for yourself.

INDEX

INDEX

WARNING TO THE READER

Neuro Linguistic Programming (NLP) represents a significant advance in the development of human choice. It places at the discretion of the skilled and balanced practitioner options for living with quality which were previously assigned variously to fate, chance, genetics, accidents and divine influence. It is important to me to explicate at least partially what I intend by the descriptive phrase, *skilled and balanced*.

The *skill* issue points to the requirement in the mastery of any interesting human skill set for a commitment to practice, the personal discipline on the part of the would-be NLP practitioner to arrange his or her own context for exploring, learning and ultimately mastering of the actual body of patterning called NLP. Success at this task identifies a learner, and the result a technician.

The *balanced* issue refers to two requirements, first, the learner's ability to integrate the skill set (mastered by the technician) into each and every area of their life, personal as well as professional. Secondly, once this integration of the technical skill set has occurred, the individual is faced with the awesome responsibility of exercising these choices with some wisdom. At this point, the caterpillar bursts the confinement of the cocoon, the technician transforms herself/himself into an artist.

All the above is a somewhat circuitous way of cautioning the would-be NLP practitioner. The world at the moment seems rather overflowing with people purporting to offer training in NLP. It is here in selecting a mentor that you, the reader, may begin to exercise one of the most crucial abilities associated with artistry in the practice of NLP—namely, that of assessing the congruency of the purported trainer. If your intuitions caution you, if you detect a discrepancy between the verbal presentation of such a person and their actual behavior and performance, keep moving and looking for an appropriate model.

If you are seriously interested in having access to quality training or business consulting applications which rest firmly on the foundation of NLP which I intended when I co-created the discipline, I invite you to contact me at:

John Grinder
QUANTUM LEAP
PO Box 67359
Scotts Valley, CA 95067-7359
TEL) 408-457-0529
FAX) 408-457-2834

Grinder & Associates
•Books

A Framework For Excellence: A Resource Manual For NLP
Charlotte Bretto Milliner
ISBN 0-929514-03-3 PB

Leaves Before The Wind
Charlotte Bretto Milliner, Judith DeLozier, John Grinder & Sylvia Topel, eds.
ISBN 1-55552-051-0 PB

**Making The Message Clear: How To Master The
Business Communication Tools That Direct Productivity,
Excellence and Power**
James Eicher
ISBN 1-55552-048-0 PB

Patterns of the Hypnotic Techniques of Milton H. Erickson, M.D., Vol. I
Richard Bandler & John Grinder
ISBN 1-55552-052-9 PB

Patterns of the Hypnotic Techniques of Milton H. Erickson, M.D., Vol. II
John Grinder, Judith DeLozier & Richard Bandler
ISBN 1-55552-053-7 PB

Precision: A New Approach To Communication
Michael McMaster & John Grinder
ISBN 1-55552-049-9 PB

Turtles All The Way Down: Prerequisites To Personal Genius
John Grinder & Judith DeLozier
ISBN 1-55552-022-7 PB

 **Grinder & Associates**
•Audio Tapes

The Syntax of Behavior Series I
Presented by John Grinder & Robert Dilts
Volume 1: States and Strategies. 8 tapes
Volume 2: Anchoring: The Oldest Mystery in NLP. 8 tapes
Volume 3: Belief Systems: Methods For Change. 8 tapes
Volume 4: A Batesonian Model For Investigation. 8 tapes

The Syntax of Behavior Series II
Presented by John Grinder & Steven Gilligan
Volume 1: Tools For Mind Mastery: Meeting Life Challenges
        With Wisdom. 6 tapes
Volume 2: Generative Personality: Enjoying The Present
        & Building The Future. 7 tapes

Advanced Modeling
Replete with exercises designed to prepare you for effective modeling. The listener is led through a series of experiences which assist to create the state highly valued in the pursuit of accelerated learning. 14 tapes

Modeling The Healing Process
This series features John Grinder leading participants through the latest exercises in NLP modeling technlogy. Methods of creating optimal states for responding to healing interventions are also demonstrated. 7 tapes

Training Trainers
Designed for experienced NLP practitioners, this series covers the topic of state preparation and presuppositions of training, including the use of metaphor and congruity requirements of the presenter. 12 tapes

Metamorphous
Advanced
Product
Services

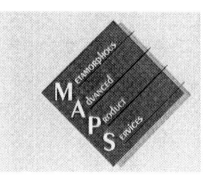

Metamorphous Advanced Product Services (M.A.P.S.) is the master distributor for Grinder & Associates and other fine publishers.

M.A.P.S. offers books, cassettes, videos, software, and miscellaneous products in the following subjects: Business & Sales, Education, Enneagram, Health, Hypnosis, Personal Development, Psychology (including Neurolinguistic Programming), and Relationships/Sexuality.

If you cannot find our books at your favorite bookstore, you can order directly from M.A.P.S.

TO ORDER OR REQUEST A FREE CATALOG:

MAIL   M.A.P.S.
P.O. Box 10616
Portland, OR 97296-0616

FAX   (503) 223-9117

CALL   Toll free 1-800-233-6277

E-MAIL metabooks@msn.com

ALL OTHER BUSINESS:

CALL   (503) 228-4972

Printed in the United States
16191LVS00001B/145

9 780929 514031